S0-ADU-340

Function Junction

The Families of Functions

Glenda Lappan, Elizabeth Difanis Phillips,
James T. Fey, Susan N. Friel

PEARSON

Boston, Massachusetts • Chandler, Arizona • Glenview, Illinois • Upper Saddle River, New Jersey

Connected Mathematics® was developed at Michigan State University with financial support from the Michigan State University Office of the Provost, Computing and Technology, and the College of Natural Science.

This material is based upon work supported by the National Science Foundation under Grant No. MDR 9150217 and Grant No. ESI 9986372. Opinions expressed are those of the authors and not necessarily those of the Foundation.

As with prior editions of this work, the authors and administration of Michigan State University preserve a tradition of devoting royalties from this publication to support activities sponsored by the MSU Mathematics Education Enrichment Fund.

Acknowledgments appear on page 118, which constitutes an extension of this copyright page.

Copyright © 2014 by Michigan State University, Glenda Lappan, Elizabeth Difanis Phillips, James T. Fey, and Susan N. Friel. Published by Pearson Education, Inc., Boston, Massachusetts 02116. All rights reserved. Printed in the United States of America. This publication is protected by copyright, and permission should be obtained from the publisher prior to any prohibited reproduction, storage in a retrieval system, or transmission in any form or by any means, electronic, mechanical, photocopying, recording, or likewise. For information regarding permission(s), write to: Rights Management & Contracts, One Lake Street, Upper Saddle River, New Jersey 07458.

Pearson, Prentice Hall, and **Pearson Prentice Hall** are trademarks, in the U.S. and/or other countries, of Pearson Education, Inc., or its affiliates.

ExamView® is a registered trademark of FSCreations, Inc.

Connected Mathematics® is a registered trademark of Pearson Education, Inc.

13-digit ISBN 978-0-13-327647-3
10-digit ISBN 0-13-327647-3
2 3 4 5 6 7 8 9 10 V011 17 16 15 14

PEARSON

Authors

A Team of Experts

Glenda Lappan is a University Distinguished Professor in the Program in Mathematics Education (PRIME) and the Department of Mathematics at Michigan State University. Her research and development interests are in the connected areas of students' learning of mathematics and mathematics teachers' professional growth and change related to the development and enactment of K–12 curriculum materials.

Elizabeth Difanis Phillips is a Senior Academic Specialist in the Program in Mathematics Education (PRIME) and the Department of Mathematics at Michigan State University. She is interested in teaching and learning mathematics for both teachers and students. These interests have led to curriculum and professional development projects at the middle school and high school levels, as well as projects related to the teaching and learning of algebra across the grades.

James T. Fey is a Professor Emeritus at the University of Maryland. His consistent professional interest has been development and research focused on curriculum materials that engage middle and high school students in problem-based collaborative investigations of mathematical ideas and their applications.

Susan N. Friel is a Professor of Mathematics Education in the School of Education at the University of North Carolina at Chapel Hill. Her research interests focus on statistics education for middle-grade students and, more broadly, on teachers' professional development and growth in teaching mathematics K–8.

With... Yvonne Grant and Jacqueline Stewart

Yvonne Grant teaches mathematics at Portland Middle School in Portland, Michigan. Jacqueline Stewart is a recently retired high school teacher of mathematics at Okemos High School in Okemos, Michigan. Both Yvonne and Jacqueline have worked on a variety of activities related to the development, implementation, and professional development of the CMP curriculum since its beginning in 1991.

Development Team

CMP3 Authors

Glenda Lappan, University Distinguished Professor, Michigan State University

Elizabeth Difanis Phillips, Senior Academic Specialist, Michigan State University

James T. Fey, Professor Emeritus, University of Maryland

Susan N. Friel, Professor, University of North Carolina – Chapel Hill

With...

Yvonne Grant, Portland Middle School, Michigan

Jacqueline Stewart, Mathematics Consultant, Mason, Michigan

In Memory of... William M. Fitzgerald, Professor (Deceased), Michigan State University, who made substantial contributions to conceptualizing and creating CMP1.

Administrative Assistant

Michigan State University
Judith Martus Miller

Support Staff

Michigan State University
Undergraduate Assistants:
Bradley Robert Corlett, Carly Fleming,
Erin Lucian, Scooter Nowak

Development Assistants

Michigan State University
Graduate Research Assistants:
Richard "Abe" Edwards, Nic Gilbertson,
Funda Gonulates, Aladar Horvath,
Eun Mi Kim, Kevin Lawrence, Jennifer
Nimtz, Joanne Philhower, Sasha Wang

Assessment Team

Maine
Falmouth Public Schools
Falmouth Middle School: Shawn Towle

Michigan
Ann Arbor Public Schools
Tappan Middle School
Anne Marie Nicoll-Turner

Portland Public Schools
Portland Middle School
Holly DeRosia, Yvonne Grant

Traverse City Area Public Schools
Traverse City East Middle School
Jane Porath, Mary Beth Schmitt

Traverse City West Middle School
Jennifer Rundio, Karrie Tufts

Ohio
Clark-Shawnee Local Schools
Rockway Middle School: Jim Mamer

Content Consultants

Michigan State University
Peter Lappan, Professor Emeritus,
Department of Mathematics

Normandale Community College
Christopher Danielson, Instructor,
Department of Mathematics & Statistics

University of North Carolina – Wilmington
Dargan Frierson, Jr., Professor, Department
of Mathematics & Statistics

Student Activities
Michigan State University
Brin Keller, Associate Professor,
Department of Mathematics

Consultants

Indiana
Purdue University
Mary Bouck, Mathematics Consultant

Michigan
Oakland Schools
Valerie Mills, Mathematics Education Supervisor
Mathematics Education Consultants:
Geraldine Devine, Dana Gosen

Ellen Bacon, Independent Mathematics Consultant

New York
University of Rochester
Jeffrey Choppin, Associate Professor

Ohio
University of Toledo
Debra Johanning, Associate Professor

Pennsylvania
University of Pittsburgh
Margaret Smith, Professor

Texas
University of Texas at Austin
Emma Trevino, Supervisor of Mathematics Programs, The Dana Center

Mathematics for All Consulting
Carmen Whitman, Mathematics Consultant

....

Reviewers

Michigan
Ionia Public Schools
Kathy Dole, Director of Curriculum and Instruction

Grand Valley State University
Lisa Kasmer, Assistant Professor

Portland Public Schools
Teri Keusch, Classroom Teacher

Minnesota
Hopkins School District 270
Michele Luke, Mathematics Coordinator

....

Field Test Sites for CMP3

Michigan
Ann Arbor Public Schools
Tappan Middle School
Anne Marie Nicoll-Turner*

Portland Public Schools
Portland Middle School: Mark Braun, Angela Buckland, Holly DeRosia, Holly Feldpausch, Angela Foote, Yvonne Grant*, Kristin Roberts, Angie Stump, Tammi Wardwell

Traverse City Area Public Schools
Traverse City East Middle School
Ivanka Baic Berkshire, Brenda Dunscombe, Tracie Herzberg, Deb Larimer, Jan Palkowski, Rebecca Perreault, Jane Porath*, Robert Sagan, Mary Beth Schmitt*

Traverse City West Middle School
Pamela Alfieri, Jennifer Rundio, Maria Taplin, Karrie Tufts*

Maine
Falmouth Public Schools
Falmouth Middle School: Sally Bennett, Chris Driscoll, Sara Jones, Shawn Towle*

Minnesota
Minneapolis Public Schools
Jefferson Community School
Leif Carlson*,
Katrina Hayek Munsisoumang*

Ohio
Clark-Shawnee Local Schools
Reid School: Joanne Gilley
Rockway Middle School: Jim Mamer*
Possum School: Tami Thomas

*Indicates a Field Test Site Coordinator

The Families of Functions

1 The Families of Functions — 7

2 Arithmetic and Geometric Sequences — 32

Looking Ahead

Taxi fares are often calculated with a function. **What** sort of graph would you expect for such a function? **What** units and scale make sense for this graph?

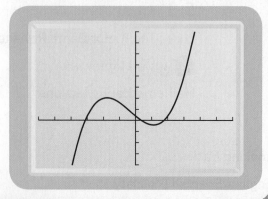

RATES

$5.00 for distances one mile or less and $2.00 for each additional mile or part of a mile

TAXI

On television quiz shows, the payoff increases for each correct answer. Suppose the pattern continues. **What** are the next five payoffs you expect?

Odd$ Are

$100

$300

$500

The graph at the right has a different shape than any of the linear, quadratic, exponential, or inverse functions you have studied before. **What** kind of algebraic function has a graph like this?

In other Units, you looked for important relationships between variables. You represented those relationships with algebraic expressions, equations, and graphs. You used those representations to solve Problems. Some of those Problems were about amusements park rides such as Bumper Cars, the Sky Dive, and wood-frame and steel-frame roller coasters.

Working on the Problems of this Unit will extend your understanding of functions and their representations. You will study new forms of mathematical notation. You will explore new families of functions and new techniques for transforming expressions to equivalent forms and solving equations. Finally, you will learn about an extension of the real number system.

Mathematical Highlights

The Families of Functions

Functions have been a major theme throughout all of your work with algebra. In *Function Junction* you will take a deeper look at functions and explore new functions.

The Investigations in this Unit will help you learn how to

- Determine the domain and range of functions and the $f(x)$ notation for expressing functions

- Examine numeric and graphic properties of step and piecewise-defined functions

- Investigate properties and uses of inverse functions

- Investigate properties and applications of arithmetic and geometric sequences

- Explore the relationships between functions with graphs connected by transformations such as translations and dilations

- Express quadratic functions in equivalent vertex form and use that new form to solve equations and sketch graphs

- Develop a formula for solving any quadratic equation

- Explore the meaning and operations of complex numbers

- Use polynomial expressions and functions to model and to answer questions about data patterns and graphs that cannot be represented with linear, quadratic, inverse variation, or exponential functions

As you work through the Problems of this Unit, it will be helpful to keep asking yourself questions such as these:

What are the variables in the situation and how are they related?

What familiar type of function could be used to model the relationship of variables, or is something new required?

How are algebraic expressions and graphs of the relationship between variables connected to each other?

How can the algebraic expression for a function be written in a form that makes it easier to sketch or analyze a graph or solve an equation?

Mathematical Practices and Habits of Mind

In the *Connected Mathematics* curriculum you will develop an understanding of important mathematical ideas by solving problems and reflecting on the mathematics involved. Every day, you will use "habits of mind" to make sense of problems and apply what you learn to new situations. Some of these habits are described by the *Common Core State Standards for Mathematical Practices* (MP).

MP1 Make sense of problems and persevere in solving them.

When using mathematics to solve a problem, it helps to think carefully about

- data and other facts you are given and what additional information you need to solve the problem;
- strategies you have used to solve similar problems and whether you could solve a related simpler problem first;
- how you could express the problem with equations, diagrams, or graphs;
- whether your answer makes sense.

MP2 Reason abstractly and quantitatively.

When you are asked to solve a problem, it often helps to

- focus first on the key mathematical ideas;
- check that your answer makes sense in the problem setting;
- use what you know about the problem setting to guide your mathematical reasoning.

MP3 Construct viable arguments and critique the reasoning of others.

When you are asked to explain why a conjecture is correct, you can

- show some examples that fit the claim and explain why they fit;
- show how a new result follows logically from known facts and principles.

When you believe a mathematical claim is incorrect, you can

- show one or more counterexamples—cases that don't fit the claim;
- find steps in the argument that do not follow logically from prior claims.

MP4 Model with mathematics.

When you are asked to solve problems, it often helps to

- think carefully about the numbers or geometric shapes that are the most important factors in the problem, then ask yourself how those factors are related to each other;
- express data and relationships in the problem with tables, graphs, diagrams, or equations, and check your result to see if it makes sense.

MP5 Use appropriate tools strategically.

When working on mathematical questions, you should always

- decide which tools are most helpful for solving the problem and why;
- try a different tool when you get stuck.

MP6 Attend to precision.

In every mathematical exploration or problem-solving task, it is important to

- think carefully about the required accuracy of results: is a number estimate or geometric sketch good enough, or is a precise value or drawing needed?
- report your discoveries with clear and correct mathematical language that can be understood by those to whom you are speaking or writing.

MP7 Look for and make use of structure.

In mathematical explorations and problem solving, it is often helpful to

- look for patterns that show how data points, numbers, or geometric shapes are related to each other;
- use patterns to make predictions.

MP8 Look for and express regularity in repeated reasoning.

When results of a repeated calculation show a pattern, it helps to

- express that pattern as a general rule that can be used in similar cases;
- look for shortcuts that will make the calculation simpler in other cases.

You will use all of the Mathematical Practices in this Unit. Sometimes, when you look at a Problem, it is obvious which practice is most helpful. At other times, you will decide on a practice to use during class explorations and discussions. After completing each Problem, ask yourself:

- What mathematics have I learned by solving this Problem?
- What Mathematical Practices were helpful in learning this mathematics?

The Families of Functions

In earlier Units you studied real-world situations that involved relationships between variables. Here are some examples:

- Distance traveled by riders on a bike tour related to the time riding
- Area of a rectangular piece of land with a fixed perimeter related to the width
- Strength of a bridge related to the length
- Area of ballots cut from a piece of paper related to the number of cuts

In each situation you asked these questions:

- What are the variable quantities?
- What measurement units are appropriate for the situation?

Common Core State Standards

F-IF.A.1 Understand that a function from one set (called the domain) to another set (called the range) assigns to each element of the domain exactly one element of the range.

F-IF.C.7b Graph square root, cube root, and piecewise-defined functions, including step functions and absolute value functions.

F-BF.B.4a Solve an equation of the form $f(x) = c$ for a simple function f that has an inverse and write an expression for the inverse.

Also N-Q.A.1, N-Q.A.2, F-IF.A.2, F-IF.B.4, F-IF.B.5, F-IF.B.6

The relationships in the examples from earlier Units are called *functions*. Some of the types of functions you studied are expressed with equations:

- Linear functions, with equations in the form $y = mx + b$
- Quadratic functions, with equations in the form $y = ax^2 + bx + c$
- Inverse variation functions, with equations in the form $y = \frac{k}{x}$
- Exponential functions, with equations in the form $y = a(b^x)$

In each case, every value of the independent variable x is related to exactly one value of the dependent variable y. Any relationship between variables with that property is called a **function**. Many functions have rules that are quite different from those that you have studied so far.

The Problems in this Investigation introduce the standard terminology and notation for functions. You will also study new families of special functions.

1.1 Filling Functions

Not all functions can be defined by simple algebraic rules. Suppose you fill each of these containers with water flowing in at a constant rate. Then you study the results.

- What variables does this situation suggest?
- What are the best units to measure the quantities involved?
- What would tables, graphs, or equations of each of the functions related to filling these containers look like?

Look at each container pictured above. The height of water at any time depends on the length of time the water has been flowing into it. There is exactly one water height at each point in time. So height is a function of time.

Problem 1.1

A Match each of these (*time, water height*) graphs to one of the containers on the preceding page. Explain why each graph shows the rate of filling for one of the containers. Assume the water flows at a constant rate.

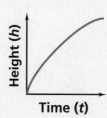
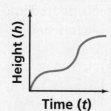
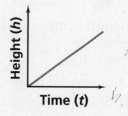

B Sketch containers that would have functions for rate of filling that would match these graphs.

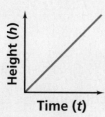
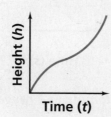
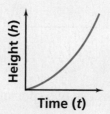

C The drawings below show a two-dimensional view of containers that have a constant dimension of 1 inch from front to back. Again, the water flows at a constant rate. Sketch graphs of the functions for rate of filling for these containers.

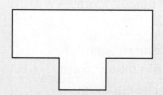
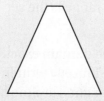
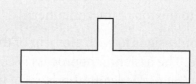

D Do the graphs in Questions A–C represent any functions you have seen in previous Units? Explain.

E Delsin and Christina are analyzing the graphs from Question C. Delsin says those graphs show volume as a function of time. Christina says that graphs showing how volume changes over time would be three identical graphs. They would be linear graphs for all three containers. She thinks the graphs show how height changes over time. Who is right? Explain.

 Homework starts on page 20.

1.2 Domain, Range, and Function Notation

The drawing below shows the side view of a lab flask that you might use in chemistry class. The graph shows how the height of water in the flask changes with time as a steady flow of water is poured into it. The relation between the *height* of the water and *time* is a function.

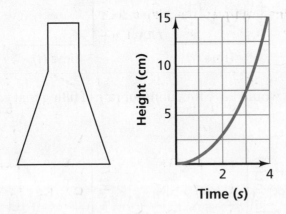

Mathematicians use two special terms, *domain* and *range*, to describe any function.

- The **domain** of a function is the set of all possible values for the input variable. For the filling function, the domain is the set of all times for which there is a related height.

- The **range** of a function is the set of all possible values for the output variable. For the filling function, the range is the set of heights from zero to the top of the container.

A function assigns to each element of the domain exactly one element of the range. The assignment process is commonly written in symbolic form. The notation $h(t)$ is read, "the value of height h at time t." The equation $h(2) = 3$ tells you that the height of the water in the flask is 3 centimeters after 2 seconds of pouring. The notation $h(t)$ does *not* mean h times t.

- What is the domain of the height function shown in the graph?

- What range makes sense for the function shown in the graph?

- What is each equation asking and what value would you insert to make it a true statement?

$h(0) = \blacksquare$ $\qquad$ $h(2) = \blacksquare$ $\qquad$ $h(\blacksquare) = 1$ $\qquad$ $h(\blacksquare) = 10$

Function notation _f(x)_ is another way of expressing rules for functions. For example, the function $y = 1.5x - 4$ can be written as $f(x) = 1.5x - 4$. The notation shows the relationships between the independent and dependent variables in a short form. The sentence $f(10) = 11$ tells you that the value of y is 11 when the value of x is 10.

Problem 1.2

A For each of the following examples, describe a domain and a range that make sense for the function. Then use function notation to complete the given sentences.

   1. a. Suppose $f(x) = 1.5x - 4$. What are the domain and range of $f(x)$?

   b. $f(3) = \blacksquare$ **c.** $f(-2) = \blacksquare$ **d.** $f(\blacksquare) = 5$

   e. $f(\blacksquare) = -1$ **f.** $f(n) = \blacksquare$ **g.** $f(x + 1) = \blacksquare$

   2. a. Suppose $g(x) = \sqrt{x}$. What are the domain and range of $g(x)$?

   b. $g(9) = \blacksquare$ **c.** $g(49) = \blacksquare$ **d.** $g(\blacksquare) = 5$

   e. $g(t) = \blacksquare$ **f.** $g(x - 5) = \blacksquare$

   3. a. Suppose $h(x) = 5(2^x)$. What are the domain and range of $h(x)$?

   b. $h(-3) = \blacksquare$ **c.** $h(0) = \blacksquare$ **d.** $h(\blacksquare) = 40$

   e. $h(m) = \blacksquare$ **f.** $h(3x) = \blacksquare$

B The graph of any function f is the set of all points with coordinates $(x, f(x))$, or the set of all points (x, y) that satisfy the equation $y = f(x)$. Sketch graphs of the three functions defined in Part A.

C Not all relationships between variables are functions. For example, the next table shows age in years and height in inches of students on a middle school basketball team.

Heights and Ages

Age (years)	11	11	12	12	12	13	13	13	13	14
Height (inches)	60	58	62	67	62	65	68	72	68	70

Why is _height_ not a function of _age_ in this case?

Ⓐ Ⓒ Ⓔ Homework starts on page 20.

1.3 Taxi Fares, Time Payments, and Step Functions

In many important applications of mathematics a function is defined in words. However, it may not be easy to write a simple algebraic expression for that function. For example, the fare for riding in a taxicab might be calculated with a function such as the one described on the cab below:

RATES

$5.00 for distances one mile or less and $2.00 for each additional mile or part of a mile

TAXI

RATES

In this taxi you would pay $5.00 for any trip 1 mile or less in length. You'd pay $7.00 for any trip longer than 1 mile but not longer than 2 miles. You'd pay $9.00 for any trip longer than 2 miles but not longer than 3 miles, and so on.

- Suppose you made a table and graph for the function relating taxicab fare to distance traveled. What patterns would you expect to see?

Analyzing relationships like the taxicab fare scheme is easier if you calculate some sample values and look for a pattern.

Problem 1.3

A 1. Complete the table at the right to show taxicab fares for trips from 1 to 8 miles.

Taxi Fares

Distance (mi)	1	2	3	4	5	6	7	8
Fare ($)	5	7	■	■	■	■	■	■

2. Graph the data points in the table of sample taxi fares. Complete the graph so it shows the fares for any distances between 0 and 8 miles.

3. Does the completed graph represent a function? If not, why not? If it does, what are its domain and range?

Problem **1.3** *continued*

B When stores want to sell things quickly, they offer deals that spread payments over many months with 0% interest. Suppose that you buy a new bicycle for $240. You get a deal that requires $10 monthly payments.

1. Complete the following table to show the unpaid balance for months 0 to 7.

Account Balance

Month	0	1	2	3	4	5	6	7
Unpaid Balance ($)	240	230	▪	▪	▪	▪	▪	▪

2. Graph the data points in the table of unpaid balances. Then complete the graph so it shows the unpaid balance at any time between 0 and 7 months.

3. Does the completed graph represent a function? If not, why not? If it does, what are its domain and range?

C In many quantitative problems it makes sense to round numbers to a nearby whole-number value. There are three common ways to do this rounding:

- The *standard rounding rule* takes the integer closest to x, with values exactly halfway between integers rounded up

- The *ceiling rule* takes the nearest integer greater than or equal to x

- The *floor rule* takes the nearest integer less than or equal to x

1. Complete the following table of values for the standard, ceiling, and floor rounding rules.

Comparing Standard, Ceiling, and Floor Functions

x	−3.25	−2.75	−0.5	0.6	1.7	2.21	3.5
Standard	▪	▪	▪	▪	▪	▪	▪
Ceiling	▪	▪	▪	▪	▪	▪	▪
Floor	▪	▪	▪	▪	▪	▪	▪

2. Pick one of the three rules and draw a graph of its values for $x = -3$ to $x = 3$.

3. Do any of the rules define functions? If not, why not? If so, what are the domain(s) and range(s)?

continued on the next page >

Problem **1.3** *continued*

D The relationships between variables that you analyzed in Questions A–C are examples of a special type of functions called **step functions.**

1. How do the graphs show why the step function name makes sense?

2. Why it is hard to give an algebraic expression for calculating values of such functions?

A C E Homework starts on page 20.

1.4 Piecewise-Defined Functions

 Suppose the container below has constant width from front to back. Water pours into it at a constant rate.

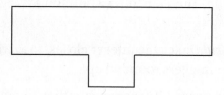

- How rapidly will the water level rise?

- What sort of graph would you expect for the function relating water height to time?

- What kind of algebraic rule would express the height function?

There is a function that describes the rate at which water fills the container pictured above. You can write rules that relate the dependent and independent variables for that function. However, the rules or expressions for that function and others like it are different on different pieces of the domain. Such relationships are called **piecewise-defined functions.**

The following Problem will enhance your understanding of piecewise-defined functions. You will work with some function rules that are stated in words and others given as algebraic expressions.

Problem 1.4

Ⓐ The graph below models the rate at which the water level would rise in the container pictured to its left.

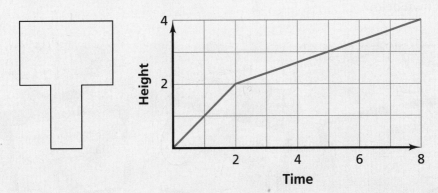

1. Why does it make sense that the graph should consist of two different linear pieces?

2. What algebraic expressions would you use to model the pieces of the rate of filling function?

Ⓑ The absolute value function has the following piecewise definition:

$$|x| = \begin{cases} x \ if \ x \geq 0 \\ -x \ if \ x < 0 \end{cases}$$

1. Copy and complete this table of values for the absolute value function $v(x) = |x|$.

x	−3	−2.5	−2	−1.5	−1	0	1	1.5	2	2.5	3
$v(x) = |x|$	3	▪	▪	▪	▪	▪	▪	▪	▪	▪	▪

2. Use the data for the points $(x, |x|)$ to draw a graph of $v(x)$.

Ⓒ Use results from Question B to draw graphs of these variations on the absolute value function.

1. $a(x) = |x| + 1$

2. $b(x) = |x| - 2$

3. $c(x) = v(x) - 1$

4. Explain how these graphs are related to the graph of $v(x) = |x|$.

continued on the next page >

Problem **1.4** *continued*

D Competitors in iron-man triathlon races swim, bicycle, and run a total of 140.6 miles. Suppose that one racer's pace in each part of the race was as shown below.

Swimming
Distance: 2.4 miles
Time: 2 hours

Biking
Distance: 112 miles
Time: 8 hours

Running
Distance: 26.2 miles
Time: 4 hours

1. What were the racer's average speeds for swimming, biking, and running?

2. Sketch a graph showing the racer's progress over the whole race. Assume that the pace on each segment of the race is constant .

3. What are the domain and range of the function graphed in part (2)?

4. Based on your graph, estimate the racer's average rate for the entire triathlon.

ACE Homework starts on page 20.

1.5 Inverse Functions

If an airplane averages 500 miles per hour in flight, you know that the time and distance traveled are related. Look at the two tables below. Numbers in the first table show distance as a function of time. Numbers in the second table show time as a function of distance.

The equations $d = 500t$ and $f(t) = 500t$ both show how distance traveled is related to time in flight.

Using units of measure helps to keep track of the domain and range. Here is an example.

2,000 miles = 500 mph $\times$ 4 hours

Time and Distance

Time (hours)	Distance (miles)
0	0
1	500
2	1,000
3	1,500
4	2,000
■	■
t	$500t$

The equations $t = d \div 500$ and $g(d) = d \div 500$ both show how time in flight is related to distance traveled.

- How do units of measure help make sense of this sentence?

  4 hours = 2,000 miles $\div$ 500 mph

Distance and Time

Distance (miles)	Time (hours)
0	0
500	1
1,000	2
1,500	3
2,000	4
■	■
d	■

The functions $f(x) = 500x$ and $g(x) = x \div 500$ are related in a very special and useful way. The function $g(x)$ is the **inverse function** of $f(x)$, and $f(x)$ is the inverse function of $g(x)$.

- Why does the term *inverse* make sense in describing how functions $f(x)$ and $g(x)$ are related?

Working on this Problem will develop your ability to find and use inverses of familiar functions.

Problem 1.5

For the situations described in Questions A–E, do the following:

- Write an equation that shows how the two variables are related.

- Use function notation to write an equation that shows the same relationship.

- Write the equation and function that show the inverse relationship of the two variables.

- Explain what the function and its inverse tell about the related variables.

A A bus averages 50 miles per hour on the highway. How is the distance covered d, in miles, related to the driving time t, in hours?

B A gas station offers the price shown in the advertisement below. How is the price per gallon on Tuesday T related to the price D on other days of the week?

GASOLINE SERVICE

100 Main Street

TUESDAYS ARE SPECIAL!

Get **20¢** off the regular price per gallon.

C The typical customer at the Spartan Deli buys food that costs $7.50. How is the Deli's daily income I related to the number of customers n?

D 1. The Spartan Deli has operating expenses of $850 per day. How is the Deli's daily profit P related to the number of customers n?

   2. Amy thinks that the answer for the inverse is $n = P \div 7.50 + 850$. Becky says that the units needed for the expression on the right side of this equation would not give a number of people. Who do you agree with? Explain.

Problem **1.5** *continued*

E How is the area A of any square related to the length s of its sides?

F For any function $f(x)$, the inverse function is shown by the function notation $f^{-1}(x)$. The notation $f^{-1}(x)$ is read, "f inverse of x."

Suppose a function $f(x)$ tells the range value corresponding to each domain value. Then the inverse of that function reverses this relationship. Values that were in the domain are now in the range, and vice versa.

Find inverses for the functions below and explain how you know that your answers are correct.

Hint: You might find it helpful to write each function as an equation using y to name the dependent variable. For example, $f(x) = 3x$ could be written as $y = 3x$. Then the task is to find an expression that shows how to calculate x when given y.

1. $f(x) = 3x$
2. $g(x) = x + 7$
3. $h(x) = 3x + 7$
4. $j(x) = x - 7$
5. $k(x) = x^2$
6. $m(x) = \frac{1}{x}$
7. $n(x) = x^3$

G For each function in Question F, do the following:

- Describe the domain and range of the function.

- Describe the domain and range of the inverse function.

- Explain any ways that the domain of the original function must be limited if it is to have the proposed inverse.

- Sketch a graph of the function and a graph of its inverse. Use separate coordinate axes for each pair of graphs.

ACE Homework starts on page 20.

Applications

1. Suppose each container below is filled at a constant rate with water. Match each container with the graph that represents the relationship between the height of the water in the container and time.

Container 1   **Container 2**   **Container 3**

Graph 1   **Graph 2**   **Graph 3**

2. The graphs below show the pattern of time and distance traveled by two school buses. Make a copy of each graph. On copies of each graph mark the following intervals:

- when the bus is speeding up

- when the bus is slowing down

- when the bus is moving at a constant speed

- when the bus is stopped

a. Bus A

b. Bus B

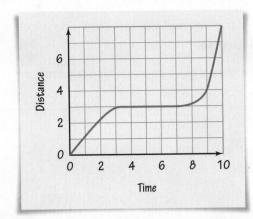

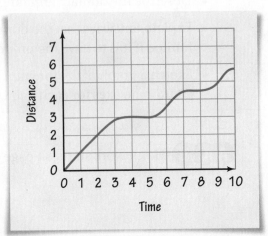

3. Ocean water levels rise and fall with a tidal period of about 12 hours. The graph below shows water depth at the end of a pier in a seacoast city.

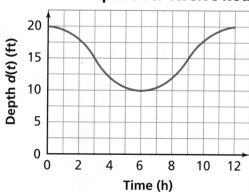

Water Depth Over Twelve Hours

The function $d(t)$ gives water depth at time t hours after midnight. Use the graph to complete the following sentences and explain what each sentence tells about water depth.

a. $d(0) = $ ▨

b. $d(2) = $ ▨

c. $d(4) = $ ▨

d. $d(6) = $ ▨

e. $d(9) = $ ▨

f. $d(■) = 15$

4. What are the domain and range of the function for water depth shown above?

Complete the sentences to give correct statements.

5. $f(x) = -2x + 5$

a. $f(7) = $ ■   b. $f(-3) = $ ■   c. $f(■) = 17$

6. $g(x) = x^2 + 5x$

a. $g(7) = $ ■   b. $g(-3) = $ ■   c. $g(■) = 6$

7. $h(x) = 4(0.5)^x$

a. $h(2) = $ ■   b. $h(-1) = $ ■   c. $h(■) = 4$

8. Describe the domain and range for the functions $f(x) = -2x + 5$, $g(x) = x^2 + 5x$, and $h(x) = 4(0.5^x)$.

9. For each function, sketch the graph and describe the domain and range.

   a. $f(x) = 4x + 5$ **b.** $g(x) = x^2 + 2$ **c.** $h(x) = 2^x$ **d.** $j(x) = \frac{1}{x}$

10. Determine if the relationship in each table shows that y is a function of x.

   a.

x	2	3	4	5	6
y	4	7	10	13	16

   b.

x	3	4	1	-1	2
y	4	3	-1	1	2

   c.

x	0	2	4	3	0
y	1	3	5	7	9

   d.

x	-4	-3	-1	1	2
y	0	1	1	1	0

For Exercises 11 and 12, use the graphs below.

$f(x)$

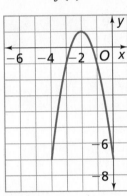

$g(x)$

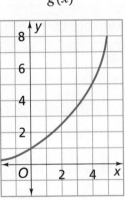

$h(x)$

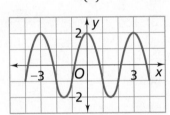

11. Identify the domain and range of each function.

12. Use the graphs to complete these sentences that use function notation.

   a. $f(-4) = \blacksquare$ **b.** $g(4) = \blacksquare$ **c.** $h(1) = \blacksquare$

   d. $f(\blacksquare) = 1$ **e.** $g(\blacksquare) = 1$ **f.** $h(\blacksquare) = 2$

13. The fee for airport parking is shown below. For parts (a)–(f), calculate the cost of parking $c(t)$ for the given times.

   a. $c(0.5)$ **b.** $c(1.0)$ **c.** $c(2.5)$

   d. $c(5.0)$ **e.** $c(5.5)$ **f.** $c(8.0)$

   g. Draw a graph showing the charges for any time from 0 to 8 hours.

14. Multiple Choice At Akihito's school, lunches cost $1.25. Akihito starts the school year with a school lunch account balance of $100. Which graph best represents the pattern of change in Akihito's account balance during a typical week?

A.

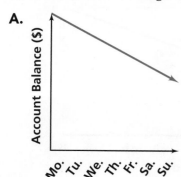

B.

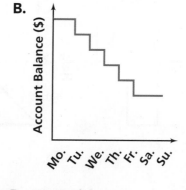

C.

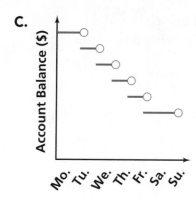

D. None of these

15. Suppose $r(x)$ is the function that applies the standard rounding rule to numbers. Also, $c(x)$ applies the ceiling rule for rounding, and $f(x)$ applies the floor rule for rounding. Complete the following sentences to give correct statements.

a. $r(1.6) = $ ▪   **b.** $c(1.6) = $ ▪   **c.** $f(1.6) = $ ▪

d. $r(-1.6) = $ ▪   **e.** $c(-1.6) = $ ▪   **f.** $f(-1.6) = $ ▪

g. $r(-1.3) = $ ▪   **h.** $c(-1.3) = $ ▪   **i.** $f(-1.3) = $ ▪

j. $r(■) = -2$ **k.** $c(■) = -2$ **m.** $f(■) = -2$

16. Graph each of the following piecewise functions.

a. $y = \begin{cases} x^2 \text{ if } x \leq 0 \\ 3x \text{ if } x > 0 \end{cases}$

b. $y = \begin{cases} \frac{1}{2}x + 4 \text{ if } x < 0 \\ -\frac{1}{2}x + 4 \text{ if } x \geq 0 \end{cases}$

c. $y = \begin{cases} 4 \text{ if } x < 2 \\ 2^x \text{ if } x \geq 2 \end{cases}$

17. The figure and graph below show the function for rate of filling for the container from Problem 1.4.

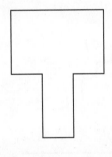
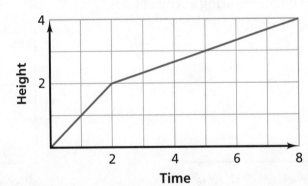

Suppose that the height of the water is measured in inches and the filling time in seconds. At what rate is water height rising during the following intervals?

a. the first two seconds

b. the time from 2 to 8 seconds

18. Desheng and Chelsea are trying to write a piecewise function rule for the following graph.

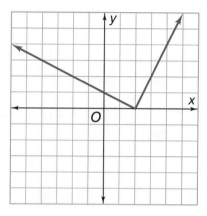

Desheng says the y-intercept is 1, the slope of the left part is $-\frac{1}{2}$, and the slope of the right part is 2. He writes the following function rule.

$$y = \left[\begin{array}{l} -\frac{1}{2}x + 1 \ if \ x < 2 \\ 2x + 1 \ if \ x \geq 2 \end{array} \right.$$

Chelsea says the left part of the graph has slope $-\frac{1}{2}$ and y-intercept of 1. The right part of the graph has slope 2. It would have a y-intercept of -4 if the graph extended to intersect the y-axis. She writes the following function rule.

$$y = \left[\begin{array}{l} -\frac{1}{2}x + 1 \ if \ x \leq 2 \\ 2x - 4 \ if \ x > 2 \end{array} \right.$$

Whose reasoning is correct? Explain.

19. Find inverses for these functions.

a. $f(x) = 6x$ **b.** $g(x) = x - 4$ **c.** $h(x) = 6x - 4$

d. $j(x) = \sqrt{x}$ **e.** $k(x) = 4x^2$ **f.** $m(x) = -\frac{3}{x}$

20. For each function in Exercise 19, do the following.

- Describe the domain and range of the function.

- Describe the domain and range of the inverse function.

- Explain any ways that the domain of the inverse function differs from the domain of original function. (In what ways must the domain of the inverse function be limited?)

Connections

21. For $f(x) = \sqrt{x}$, evaluate each of the following.

  a. $f(121)$ **b.** $f\left(\frac{1}{4}\right)$ **c.** $f(m^2)$ **d.** $f\left(4q^2\right)$

22. For $f(x) = 4^x$, complete the following sentences.

  a. $f(4) = \blacksquare$ **b.** $f(-2) = \blacksquare$ **c.** $f(\blacksquare) = 1$

  d. $f(\blacksquare) = 2$ **e.** $f(a) = \blacksquare$ **f.** $f(b + 2) = \blacksquare$

23. For $g(x) = x^2$, evaluate each of the following expressions.

  a. $g(3)$ **b.** $g\left(\frac{1}{2}\right)$ **c.** $g(-d)$ **d.** $g\left(\frac{n}{2m}\right)$

24. For $j(x) = \frac{1}{2}x$, evaluate each of the following expressions.

  a. $j(-7)$ **b.** $j(0)$ **c.** $j(2s)$ **d.** $j\left(\frac{r}{t}\right)$

25. Linear, quadratic, and exponential functions all have as their domains the set of real numbers.

  a. Why is the domain of $r(x) = \sqrt{x}$ not all real numbers?

  b. Why is the domain of $s(x) = \frac{1}{x}$ not all real numbers?

26. Many variables in your life change as time passes. Tell whether any of the following changes shows a pattern like a step function. **Hint:** More than one pattern may be a step function.

  a. your height

  b. the price of a one-scoop cone of ice cream

  c. your age in years

  d. the number of questions left to answer as you work on homework

27. For each of the following numeric equations, write the other equations in the fact family.

  a. $7 + 12 = 19$

  b. $4 \times 3 = 12$

28. Addition and subtraction are inverse operations. Multiplication and division are also inverse operations. How do those inverse operation labels relate to the inverse functions in Problem 1.5?

29. Solve each of these equations using ideas about fact families and inverse operations.

  a. $x + 7 = 12$

  b. $5x = 35$

  c. $5x + 7 = 82$

  d. $\frac{7}{x} = 12$

  e. $\frac{9}{x - 2} = 3$

  f. $\frac{5}{x} + 7 = 8$

Extensions

30. a. Copy and complete the following table of values.

Variations of the Ceiling Rounding Function $c(x)$

x	0	0.25	0.5	0.75	1.0	1.25	1.5	1.75	2.0	2.25	2.5
$c(x) - x$	■	■	■	■	■	■	■	■	■	■	■
$x - c(x)$	■	■	■	■	■	■	■	■	■	■	■

  b. Using data in the table, draw a graph of $c(x) - c$ from $x = 0$ to $x = 5$.

  c. Using data in the table, draw a graph of $c - c(x)$ from $x = 0$ to $x = 5$.

  d. What can you conclude from the two graphs?

31. a. Copy and complete the following table of values.

Variations of the Floor Rounding Function $f(x)$

x	0	0.25	0.5	0.75	1.0	1.25	1.5	1.75	2.0	2.25	2.5
$f(x) - x$	■	■	■	■	■	■	■	■	■	■	■
$x - f(x)$	■	■	■	■	■	■	■	■	■	■	■

  b. Using data in the table, draw a graph of $f(x) - f$ from $x = 0$ to $x = 5$.

  c. Using data in the table, draw a graph of $f - f(x)$ from $x = 0$ to $x = 5$.

  d. What can you conclude from the two graphs?

32. What are the domain and range of the ceiling function $c(x)$?

33. Sketch graphs for each of these pairs of functions for $x = 0$ to $x = 5$. Draw the line $y = x$ on each graph. Then describe the relationship of the pair of inverse function graphs to the $y = x$ line.

    a. $f(x) = 2x$ and $g(x) = 0.5x$

    b. $h(x) = x^2$ and $j(x) = \sqrt{x}$

34. Describe functions with these domains and ranges.

    a. domain: all real numbers
        range: all real numbers greater than or equal to zero

    b. domain: all real numbers
        range: all integers

    c. domain: all nonnegative real numbers
        range: all nonpositive real numbers

35. Connie and Margaret are given the following extra credit problem: For $g(x) = 2x + 4$, find $g(g(1))$.

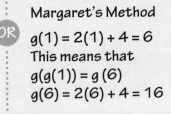

Connie's Method

$g(g(1))$ is the same as $(g(1))^2$
So, $g(1) = 2(1) + 4 = 6$
which means that
$(g(1))^2 = 6^2 = 36$.

OR

Margaret's Method

$g(1) = 2(1) + 4 = 6$
This means that
$g(g(1)) = g(6)$
$g(6) = 2(6) + 4 = 16$

    Which of these methods is correct? Explain.

36. a. Suppose $f(x) = 5x + 35$ and $g(x) = 5(2^x)$. Find the point where the graphs of $y = f(x)$ and $y = g(x)$ intersect.

    b. Explain why the x-coordinates of the points where the graphs of the equations $y = f(x)$ and $y = g(x)$ intersect are the solutions of the equation $f(x) = g(x)$.

37. Scott and Jim are driving from Gilbertville to Rivertown. The cities are 30 miles apart. Halfway between them is an intersection with the road east to Delmore City. You can see Scott and Jim's route on the diagram below. They are traveling at 60 mph (miles per hour).

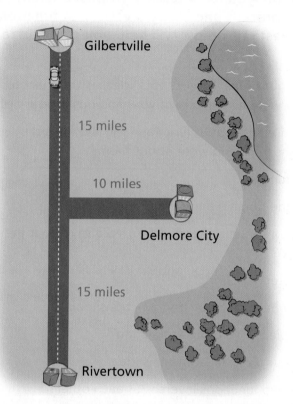

Gilbertville

15 miles

10 miles

Delmore City

15 miles

Rivertown

a. Suppose that Scott and Jim measure distance in miles along the roads shown and time in minutes. Write a piecewise function rule for the function relating distance d from Delmore City to time t.

b. Draw a graph that shows how far they are from Delmore City at any time in their trip from Gilbertville to Rivertown.

c. Suppose that you measure distance "as the crow flies," rather than along the roads that are shown. How would that change the function rule and graph?

In this Investigation, you used tables, graphs, and algebraic expressions to represent and study a variety of functions relating variables. The questions below will help you summarize what you have learned.

Think about these questions. Discuss your ideas with other students and your teacher. Then write a summary of your findings in your notebook.

1. This Investigation was about functions and the ways that mathematicians think and write about them.

   a. **What** is a function?

   b. **What** are the domain and range of a function?

   c. **What** does a statement such as $f(6) = 23$ say about the function $f(x)$?

2. a. **What** is a step function?

   b. **Describe** what graphs of step functions look like.

3. a. **What** is a piecewise-defined function?

   b. **Give** an example to illustrate this idea.

4. a. **When** are two functions inverses of each other?

   b. **What** example would you give to illustrate this idea?

Common Core Mathematical Practices

As you worked on the Problems in this Investigation, you used prior knowledge to make sense of them. You also applied Mathematical Practices to solve the Problems. Think back over your work, the ways you thought about the Problems, and how you used Mathematical Practices.

Tori described her thoughts in the following way:

In Problem 2 of this Investigation, we learned how to use the terms *domain* and *range*. They describe the possible values for independent and dependent variables in a relationship.

We learned how to use *f*(x) notation to specify rules for functions and values to be calculated.

We also learned how the terms *step function* and *piecewise function* explain the patterns of change in those kinds of relationships.

....

Common Core Standards for Mathematical Practice
MP6 Attend to precision.

- What other Mathematical Practices can you identify in Tori's reasoning?

- Describe a Mathematical Practice that you and your classmates used to solve a different Problem in this Investigation.

Arithmetic and Geometric Sequences

Quiz shows have long been a popular feature of television programming. In most such shows, the payoff for correct answers increases as the difficulty of questions increases.

Here are payoff patterns from two different shows. The payoffs on *Odds Are* increase from $100 to $300 to $500 to $700 to $900 and so on. The payoffs on *Double or Nothing* increase from $50 to $100 to $200 to $400 to $800 and so on.

- If the patterns in those examples continue, what are the next five payoffs you would expect for each game?

- Which game do you think would give the greater total payoff if a contestant got ten straight questions correct?

. . . .

Common Core State Standards

F-IF.A.3 Recognize that sequences are functions, sometimes defined recursively, whose domain is a subset of the integers.

F-BF.A.1a. Determine an explicit expression, a recursive process, or steps for calculation from a context.

F-BF.A.2 Write arithmetic and geometric sequences both recursively and with an explicit formula, use them to model situations, and translate between the two forms.

Also F-IF.A.2, F-LE.A.2

You probably recognize that the two quiz show payoff schemes look like the outputs of linear and exponential functions. In these examples, the domains of the functions are restricted to the whole numbers 1, 2, 3, 4, . . . Mathematicians call such special functions **sequences.**

The number patterns that occur in the quiz show payoff schemes are examples of *arithmetic sequences* and *geometric sequences.* Understanding sequences will develop your ability to recognize these special number patterns. You will also learn to express them as functions, and to use the functions for solving problems.

2.1 Arithmetic Sequences

The payoff scheme for the *Odds Are* game begins an **arithmetic sequence.** It can be modeled with a function $a(n)$ having a domain that is the whole numbers 1, 2, 3, 4, . . . The numbers in the sequence are called *terms.*

Note on Notation For example, in the sequence 100, 300, 500, 700, 900, . . . the fourth term is $a(4) = 700$. The term $a(n)$ is called the nth term, and $a(n + 1)$ is the next term. In this example, $a(n+1)$ is obtained by adding 200 to $a(n)$.

In a sequence, the value of a term can be determined from the previous term. Generating each term of a sequence from the previous term is called a *recursive* process.

- What are the key properties of arithmetic sequences?
- How are arithmetic sequences related to linear functions?

In the following Problem, look for patterns relating each term of an arithmetic sequence to the next. Then try to find a way of calculating any term in such a sequence.

Problem 2.1

Ⓐ 1. Copy and complete the table below. Follow the linear function pattern suggested by the first five values of $a(n)$.

Odds Are Payoff Function

n	1	2	3	4	5	6	7	8	9	10
a(n)	100	300	500	700	900	■	■	■	■	■

2. What is the relationship between each term in the sequence and the next? Express the relationship as an equation relating each term $a(n)$ and the next term $a(n+1)$.

3. What algebraic expression shows how to calculate $a(n)$ for any value of n, without finding every term in the sequence?

4. How are the answers to parts (1) and (2) related to each other?

Ⓑ Adsila applied for a summer job at a snack bar. The boss told her, "You will get better at the job with experience. So the hourly pay will increase steadily." He showed her this table.

Snack Bar Wages

Week n	1	2	3	4	5	6	7	8	9	10
Hourly Wage p(n)	$5.00	$5.50	$6.00	$6.50	$7.00	■	■	■	■	■

1. Complete the table of values for the hourly pay function $p(n)$. Follow the linear function pattern suggested by the first five values.

2. What is the relationship between each term in the sequence and the next? Express the relationship as an equation relating $p(n)$ and $p(n+1)$.

3. What expression shows how to calculate $p(n)$ for any n, without finding every term in the sequence?

4. How are the answers to parts (2) and (3) related to each other?

Problem 2.1 *continued*

C In Problem 1.3 you studied the way monthly payments of $10 reduce an amount owed. The payments were for a bicycle that cost $240. The amounts owed $d(n)$ form a sequence that begins 240, 230, 220, . . . So terms in the sequence are $d(1) = 240$, $d(2) = 230$, and so on.

1. What is the relationship between each term in the sequence and the next? Express the relationship as an equation relating $d(n)$ and $d(n + 1)$.

2. What expression shows how to calculate $d(n)$ for any value of n, without finding every term in the sequence?

3. How are the answers to parts (1) and (2) related to each other?

D The following tables show number patterns that are arithmetic sequences. In each case, do the following.

- Complete the table of values for the function in a way that continues the linear pattern.

- Describe the relationship between each term and the next in the sequence. Then write an equation to show that relationship.

- Write an algebraic expression that shows how to calculate the nth term in the sequence.

- Explain how the equation for the nth term in the sequence is connected to the equation that relates term n to term $(n + 1)$.

1.

n	1	2	3	4	5	6	7	8	9	10
j(n)	−7	−5	−3	−1	1	▪	▪	▪	▪	▪

2.

n	1	2	3	4	5	6	7	8	9	10
g(n)	$\frac{1}{2}$	$\frac{2}{3}$	$\frac{5}{6}$	1	$\frac{7}{6}$	▪	▪	▪	▪	▪

3.

n	1	2	3	4	5	6	7	8	9	10
h(n)	−1	0.75	2.50	4.25	6.00	▪	▪	▪	▪	▪

continued on the next page >

Problem 2.1 *continued*

E Consider properties shared by the sequences in Questions A–D.

 1. What kind of equation relates $f(n + 1)$ and $f(n)$ in each case?

 2. What kind of expression shows how to calculate $f(n)$ directly in each case?

 3. How are the answers to parts (1) and (2) related to each other?

 4. How would you define an arithmetic sequence?

F Not all number patterns are arithmetic sequences.

 1. On another television quiz show, the payoffs in the first part of the game are as follows:

    $100, $500, $1,000, $2,000, $3,000, $5,000, $7,000, $10,000, $15,000, and $25,000

    How is this sequence of numbers different from the sequences in Questions A–D?

 2. The lines on a football field are 10 yards apart. The marking on each line is the distance to the nearest goal line. After a muddy football game, a field looks like this drawing.

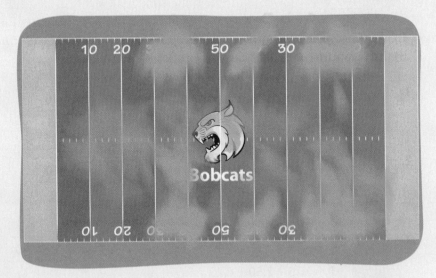

    The yard line markers start from one goal line 10, 20, 30, 40, 50, . . . How does this sequence continue? How is the resulting pattern different from the examples in Questions A–D?

 Homework starts on page 41.

2.2 Geometric Sequences

The payoffs for the *Double or Nothing* quiz show are 50, 100, 200, 400, 800, . . . The sequence is an example of a **geometric sequence**. It also can be modeled with an exponential function $g(n)$ having a domain that is the whole numbers 1, 2, 3, 4, . . . As you examine situations that involve geometric sequences, ask yourself these questions:

- What are the key properties of geometric sequences?
- How are geometric sequences related to exponential functions?

In the following Problem, look for a pattern relating each term of the sequence to the next. Then find a way to calculate any term in the sequence.

Problem 2.2

 1. Copy and complete this table of values for the function $g(n)$. Use the exponential pattern shown by the first five values of $g(n)$.

n	1	2	3	4	5	6	7	8	9	10
g(n)	50	100	200	400	800	▪	▪	▪	▪	▪

2. Daniela answers the fifteenth question correctly. What is her payoff?

3. What is the relationship between each term in the sequence and the next? That is, what equation relates $g(n)$ and $g(n + 1)$ in every case?

4. What expression shows how to calculate $g(n)$ for any value of n, without finding every term in the sequence?

5. How are the answers to parts (1) and (2) related to each other?

continued on the next page >

Problem 2.2 *continued*

B Jakayla applies for a summer job at a swimming pool. The manager wants workers who stay the whole season. So the hourly pay increases each week as shown in the table.

Swimming Pool Wages

Week n	1	2	3	4	5	6	7	8	9	10
Hourly Wage $p(n)$	$2.00	$3.00	$4.50	$6.75	▪	▪	▪	▪	▪	▪

1. Copy and complete the table of values for the hourly pay function $p(n)$. Use the exponential pattern that you think the manager has in mind.

2. What is the relationship between each term in the sequence and the next? That is, what equation relates $p(n)$ and $p(n + 1)$ in every case?

3. What expression shows how to calculate $p(n)$ for any value of n?

4. How are the answers to parts (3) and (4) related to each other?

C Suppose a sports tournament has 128 teams at the start. In each round, half the teams are eliminated. The number of teams remaining in each round is a sequence. That sequence is shown in the table below.

Teams in Tournament

Round n	1	2	3	4	5	6	7
Teams $t(n)$	128	64	32	▪	▪	▪	▪

1. Complete the table to show the number of teams in rounds 4 through 7. In which round is the championship game played?

2. What is the relationship between each term in the sequence and the next? That is, what equation relates $t(n)$ and $t(n + 1)$ in every case?

3. What expression shows how to calculate $t(n)$ for any value of n?

4. How are the sequence properties in parts (2) and (3) related to each other?

Problem 2.2 *continued*

D The following number patterns are the beginnings of geometric sequences. In each case, do the following.

- Copy and complete the table of values for the function. Continue the pattern shown by the first five entries.

- Describe the relationship between each term and the next in the sequence. Then write an equation to show that relationship.

- Write an equation that shows how to calculate any term in the sequence.

- Explain how the equation for the nth term in the sequence is connected to the equation that relates term n to term $(n + 1)$.

1.

n	1	2	3	4	5	6	7	8
$f(n)$	−1	−3	−9	−27	−81	■	■	■

2.

n	1	2	3	4	5	6	7	8
$g(n)$	2	$\frac{4}{3}$	$\frac{8}{9}$	$\frac{16}{27}$	$\frac{32}{81}$	■	■	■

3.

n	1	2	3	4	5	6	7	8	9	10
$h(n)$	−1	2	−4	8	−16	■	■	■	■	■

E Describe properties shared by the geometric sequences in Questions A–D.

1. What kind of equation relates $f(n + 1)$ and $f(n)$ in each case?

2. What kind of expression shows how to calculate $f(n)$ directly in each case?

3. How are the sequence properties in parts (1) and (2) related to each other?

4. How would you define a geometric sequence?

continued on the next page >

Problem 2.2 *continued*

F The number pattern that starts 1, 1, 2, 3, 5, 8, 13, 21, 34, 55, . . . is known to mathematicians as the *Fibonacci Sequence*. It is named after an Italian mathematician who lived more than 800 years ago.

    1. Explain why the Fibonacci numbers are neither an arithmetic sequence nor a geometric sequence.

    2. Study the pattern shown above and calculate the next five terms of the Fibonacci Sequence.

    3. As given above, the first two terms of the Fibonacci Sequence are $f(1) = 1$ and $f(2) = 1$. Complete the equation $f(n) = \blacksquare$ to show how any other term $f(n)$ of the Fibonacci Sequence can be calculated.

A C E Homework starts on page 41.

Did You Know?

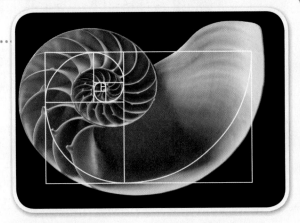

The name *Fibonacci* means "son of Bonacci." Leonardo Fibonacci was an Italian businessman who lived from about 1170 to 1250. He traveled widely through Greece and the Middle East. In his travels he picked up many ideas from Indian and Arabic mathematics.

Fibonacci published those ideas in a 1202 book titled *Liber abbaci*. There he described methods for base-ten numeration, arithmetic algorithms, and the solution of algebraic problems.

The Fibonacci Sequence was used as an early model for how some things in nature grow. For example, the Fibbonacci Sequence can be seen in the growth of a chambered nautilus shell.

Applications

For each arithmetic sequence in Exercises 1–3, do the following.

    a. Complete the table.

    b. Write the equation that relates each term $a(n)$ to the next term $a(n + 1)$.

    c. Write the algebraic expression that shows how to calculate $a(n)$ for any n, without finding the previous terms.

1.

n	1	2	3	4	5	6	7	8	9	10
a(n)	275	310	345	380	▨	▨	▨	▨	▨	▨

2.

n	1	2	3	4	5	6	7	8	9	10
a(n)	$\frac{1}{4}$	$\frac{5}{8}$	1	$\frac{11}{8}$	▨	▨	▨	▨	▨	▨

3.

n	1	2	3	4	5	6	7	8	9	10
a(n)	68	▨	▨	26	▨	−2	▨	▨	▨	▨

4. Latrell volunteers at a local charity. The first week he works a total of 2 hours (for training). Each week after the first, he volunteers $3\frac{1}{2}$ hours.

Suppose $t(n)$ represents the total number of hours worked during weeks 1 through n.

    a. Write an equation that represents the relationship between $t(n)$ and $t(n + 1)$.

    b. How many hours does Latrell volunteer in 1 year (52 weeks)?

5. An arithmetic sequence can be represented with this equation:
$a(n + 1) = 12 + a(n)$. For $n = 5$, $a(5) = 72$. What is $a(0)$? What is $a(10)$?

6. The algebraic expression $4n + 2$ represents the value of the nth term in an arithmetic sequence. What equation relates $a(n)$ and $a(n + 1)$?

For Exercises 7–16, study each number pattern to see if it begins an arithmetic sequence, a geometric sequence, or neither. For those that begin either an arithmetic sequence or a geometric sequence, do the following.

- **Tell which type of sequence, arithmetic or geometric, is shown**

- **Write an equation relating $s(n)$ and $s(n + 1)$**

- **Write an algebraic expression for a function $s(n)$ that shows how to find any term in the sequence beyond those already given**

7. $-5, 1, 7, 13, 19, 25, 31, \ldots$

8. $16, 13, 10, 7, 4, 1, -2, \ldots$

9. $10, 8, 6, 4, 2, 0, 0, 0, \ldots$

10. $5, -10, 20, -40, 80, -160, \ldots$

11. $3, 4.5, 6, 7.5, 9, 10.5, 12, \ldots$

12. $3, 2, 1, 0, 1, 2, 3, 2, 1, \ldots$

13. $27, 18, 12, 8, \frac{16}{3}, \frac{32}{9}, \frac{64}{27}, \ldots$

14. $4, 4, 4, 4, 4, \ldots$

15. $1, -1, 1, -1, 1, -1, 1, \ldots$

16. $1, 5, 25, 125, 625, 3125, \ldots$

For Exercises 17–21, answer the question that is asked. Then study each number pattern that satisfies the given conditions. For those that are arithmetic or geometric sequences, do the following.

- State whether the sequence is arithmetic or geometric
- Write an equation relating $s(n)$ and $s(n + 1)$
- Write an algebraic expression for a function $s(n)$ that shows how to find any term in the sequence
- Explain how the equation for the nth term in the sequence is connected to the equation that relates term n to term $(n + 1)$

17. On a game show, payoffs for correct responses in each question category increase as follows: $200, $400, $600, $800, $1,000. What is the total amount of money that can be won by correct answers for all questions of a category?

18. When two rivals played a round of golf they agreed to the following payoff sequence. The winner of the first hole earns 5 cents. The winner of the next hole wins 10 cents. The payoff doubles for each hole thereafter. What is the payoff for winning the 18th hole?

19. An airplane cruising at an altitude of 40,000 feet begins its descent to land. It loses altitude at a rate of 1,500 feet per minute. How long will it take to reach the ground?

20. On a 100-point multiple-choice test, the point value of each question depends on the number of questions. The 100 points are divided equally among the questions. For example, on a test with two questions, each question counts for 50 points. How many questions are on a test if each question counts for 5 points?

21. Hana wins $10,000 in the lottery. She puts the money in a bank account that pays interest of 5% once each year. How long will it take that account to grow to $20,000?

Connections

22. The sequence of prime numbers begins 2, 3, 5, 7, . . .
Suppose $p(n)$ is the nth prime number.

   a. What are $p(10)$ and $p(15)$?

   b. For what value of n is $p(n) = 41$?

   c. Is the sequence of prime numbers an arithmetic sequence, a geometric sequence, or neither?

23. Look for a pattern in this sequence of fractions: $\frac{1}{2}, \frac{2}{3}, \frac{3}{4}, \frac{4}{5}, \frac{5}{6}, \frac{6}{7}, \ldots$

   a. What are the values of $f(10)$ and $f(15)$?

   b. What expression for the function $f(n)$ will generate the fractions in the pattern for any whole number n?

   c. For what value of n is $f(n) = \frac{23}{24}$?

   d. Is the sequence of fractions an arithmetic sequence, a geometric sequence, or neither?

24. Study the sequence of decimal place values that begins
0.0001, 0.001, 0.01, 0.1, 1, 10, 100, 1,000, . . .

   a. Is the sequence of numbers an arithmetic sequence, a geometric sequence, or neither?

   b. What expression for the function $d(n)$ will generate the numbers in the pattern for any whole number n?

25. The sum of degree measures for interior angles of a convex polygon is given by a linear equation. For a polygon with n sides, that equation is $s(n) = 180(n - 2)$ for $n = 3, 4, 5, \ldots$

   a. What are the values of $s(3)$, $s(4)$, $s(5)$, and $s(6)$?

   b. Is the sequence of angle sums an arithmetic sequence, a geometric sequence, or neither?

   c. Find $s(1)$ and $s(2)$. Explain why these values make sense in the sequence of numbers but do not make sense for polygons.

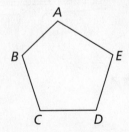

For a pentagon,
$m\angle A + m\angle B + m\angle C + m\angle D + m\angle E = 180°(n - 2)$
$= 540°$

26. Determine whether each function family will generate arithmetic sequences when their domains are restricted to the positive integers 1, 2, 3, 4, 5, . . . ?

  a. linear functions $f(x) = mx + b$

  b. quadratic functions $g(x) = ax^2 + bx + c$

  c. exponential functions $h(x) = a(b^x)$

  d. inverse variation functions $j(x) = \frac{k}{x}$

  e. Which types of functions will generate geometric sequences when their domains are restricted to the positive integers 1, 2, 3, 4, 5, . . . ?

Extensions

27. One way to determine whether a pattern might be a geometric sequence is to look at the ratio of successive terms $\frac{f(n)}{f(n-1)}$.

  a. Copy the table below and calculate ratios to complete it. Give answers as decimals accurate to 2 places.

Ratios for Terms of the Fibonacci Sequence

n	1	2	3	4	5	6	7	8	9	10
$f(n)$	1	1	2	3	5	8	13	21	34	55
$\frac{f(n)}{f(n-1)}$	■	■	■	■	■	■	■	■	■	■

  b. Mathematicians have proven that as terms of the Fibonacci Sequence continue, the ratio $\frac{f(n)}{f(n-1)}$ gets closer and closer to the number $\frac{1 + \sqrt{5}}{2}$. This number is called the *golden ratio*. Do your results in part (a) support that claim?

28. A sequence begins 1, 2, . . . and obeys the equation $g(n) = g(n-1) - g(n-2)$. Find the first 10 terms of the sequence.

In the Odds Are quiz show your total payoff will be the sum of the payoffs for all questions answered correctly. For example, if you answer the first three questions correctly, your payoff will be

$$S_3 = 100 + 300 + 500 \quad \text{so} \quad S_3 = a_1 + a_2 + a_3$$

For any sequences with terms $a_1 + a_2 + a_3, \ldots$ there is a related sequence of partial sums $S_1, S_2, S_3, \ldots$ defined in the same way.

29. For each arithmetic sequence in parts (a)–(c), write seven terms of the associated sequence of partial sums. Then tell whether that sequence of partial sums is an arithmetic sequence or some other familiar type of sequence.

    a. 1, 2, 3, 4, 5, 6, 7, . . .

    b. 5, 10, 15, 20, 25, 30, 35, . . .

    c. 20, 15, 10, 5, 0, −5, −10, . . .

    d. The sum of the first n terms of any arithmetic sequence is given by the formula $S_n = \left(\frac{n}{2}\right)(a_1 + a_n)$. Use the formula to find the sum of the first seven terms in each arithmetic sequence of parts (a)–(c). Compare your results from using the formula with your results from adding the first seven terms.

30. For each geometric sequence in parts (a)–(c), write seven terms of the associated sequence of partial sums. Then tell whether that sequence of partial sums is a geometric sequence or some other familiar type of sequence.

    a. 1, 2, 4, 8, 16, 32, 64, . . .

    b. 729, 243, 81, 27, 9, 3, 1, . . .

    c. 1, −2, 4, −8, 16, −32, 64, . . .

    d. The sum of the first n terms of any geometric sequence is given by the formula $S_n = a_1\left(\frac{1 - r^n}{1 - r}\right)$. In this formula, the first term is a_1, and the common ratio r relates successive terms. Use the formula to find the sum of the first seven terms in each geometric sequence of parts (a)–(c). Compare your results from using the formula with your results from adding the first seven terms.

Mathematical Reflections 2

In this Investigation, you studied a variety of number patterns that were examples of arithmetic and geometric sequences. The questions below will help you summarize what you have learned.

Think about these questions. Discuss your ideas with other students and your teacher. Then write a summary of your findings in your notebook.

1. **a. Describe** the defining properties of an arithmetic sequence.

   b. What examples would you give to illustrate the idea for someone?

2. **a. Describe** the defining properties of a geometric sequence.

   b. What examples would you give to illustrate the idea for someone?

3. **How** are arithmetic and geometric sequences related to linear and exponential functions?

Common Core Mathematical Practices

As you worked on the Problems in this Investigation, you used prior knowledge to make sense of them. You also applied Mathematical Practices to solve the Problems. Think back over your work, the ways you thought about the Problems, and how you used Mathematical Practices.

Nick described his thoughts in the following way:

When we worked with the number sequence $-100, 100, 300, 500, \ldots$ it helped to model the pattern in two ways.

The equation $a(n + 1) - a(n) = 200$ showed the constant difference between terms.
The equation $a(n) = -300 + 200n$ showed the same constant difference and the first term.

....

Common Core Standards for Mathematical Practice
MP4 Model with mathematics.

- What other Mathematical Practices can you identify in Nick's reasoning?

- Describe a Mathematical Practice that you and your classmates used to solve a different Problem in this Investigation.

Investigation 3

Transforming Graphs, Equations, and Functions

In earlier work you have studied many examples of quadratic functions. Their rules used a variety of algebraic expressions in the form $ax^2 + bx + c$. The following diagram shows graphs of several examples, including a simple quadratic function, $f(x) = x^2$. All quadratic function graphs and expressions can be produced by transformations of the graph and expression for the function $f(x) = x^2$.

Four Quadratic Functions

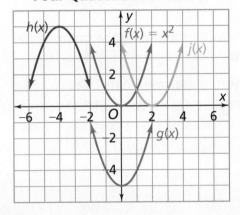

The Problems of this Investigation will develop your ability to apply transformations for quadratic functions. These transformations can be applied to other important families of functions. The explanations of how the equations and graphs transform will draw on what you know about geometric transformations and their coordinate rules.

Common Core State Standards

F-IF.C.7a Graph linear and quadratic functions and show intercepts, maxima, and minima.

F-IF.C.9 Compare properties of two functions each represented in a different way (algebraically, graphically, numerically, in tables, or by verbal descriptions).

F-BF.B.3 Identify the effect on the graph of replacing $f(x)$ by $f(x) + k$, $k\,f(x)$, $f(kx)$, and $f(x + k)$ for specific values of k (both positive and negative); find the value of k given the graphs. Experiment with cases and illustrate an explanation of the effects on the graph using technology.

Also A-SSE.B.3b, F-IF.B.4

3.1 Sliding Up and Down
Vertical Translations of Functions

The next diagram shows graphs of three functions. Their graphs are related to each other by translation up and down.

Three Quadratic Functions

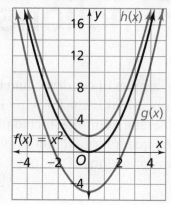

 • What are the coordinate rules for translating the graph of $f(x)$ onto the graphs of $g(x)$ and $h(x)$?

• Can you use information from these coordinate rules to write algebraic expressions for calculating values of $g(x)$ and $h(x)$?

 Problem **3.1**

A Complete a table of sample values for the functions $f(x)$, $g(x)$, and $h(x)$ graphed above.

Values for Three Quadratic Functions

x	−4	−3	−2	−1	0	1	2	3	4
$f(x) = x^2$	16	9	4	▪	▪	▪	▪	▪	▪
$g(x)$	▪	▪	▪	▪	▪	▪	▪	▪	▪
$h(x)$	▪	▪	▪	▪	▪	▪	▪	▪	▪

Problem 3.1 *continued*

B Write rules for translations that map the graph of $f(x) = x^2$ onto the other two graphs.

1. $f(x) \rightarrow g(x)$ has rule $(x, y) \rightarrow (\blacksquare, \blacksquare)$.

2. $f(x) \rightarrow h(x)$ has rule $(x, y) \rightarrow (\blacksquare, \blacksquare)$.

C Based on the results of your work in Questions A and B:

1. What algebraic expression shows how to calculate values for $g(x)$?

2. What algebraic expression shows how to calculate values for $h(x)$?

D This diagram shows graphs of four linear functions, including $f(x) = x$.

Four Linear Functions

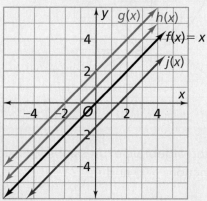

For $g(x)$, $h(x)$, and $j(x)$:

- Write the rule for the translation that maps the graph of $f(x) = x$ onto it.

- Write an algebraic expression that shows how to calculate values for the second function.

E Suppose that you are studying two functions $f(x)$ and $g(x)$. Using the rule $(x, y) \rightarrow (x, y + k)$, you can translate $f(x)$ onto $g(x)$. What equation relates the values of $f(x)$ and $g(x)$ for all values of x?

A C E Homework starts on page 58.

3.2 Stretching and Flipping Up and Down
Multiplicative Transformations of Functions

Suppose that you transformed the graph of $y = x^2$ by mapping each point (x, y) to the image point (x, ky). The image graph would be related to the original graph. The next diagram shows graphs of two quadratic functions related to $f(x) = x^2$ in that way.

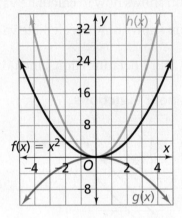

? Can you see a way to find algebraic expressions for calculating output values of the functions $g(x)$ and $h(x)$?

Study the functions in the diagram. Think about how stretching or shrinking a graph vertically changes its algebraic expression. Compare the new algebraic expression to the old expression.

Problem 3.2

Ⓐ Complete a table of sample values for the functions $f(x)$, $g(x)$, and $h(x)$ graphed above.

x	−4	−3	−2	−1	0	1	2	3	4
$f(x) = x^2$	16	9	4	1	0	1	4	9	16
$g(x)$	■	■	■	■	0	■	■	■	■
$h(x)$	■	■	■	■	0	■	■	■	■

Problem 3.2 *continued*

B Write rules that map $f(x) = x^2$ onto the other graphs.

1. $f(x) \rightarrow g(x)$ has rule $(x, y) \rightarrow (\blacksquare, \blacksquare)$.

2. $f(x) \rightarrow h(x)$ has rule $(x, y) \rightarrow (\blacksquare, \blacksquare)$.

C Based on the results of your work in Questions A and B:

1. What algebraic expression could you use for calculating values of $g(x)$?

2. What algebraic expression could you use for calculating values of $h(x)$?

D The graph of a piecewise-defined function $s(t)$ is shown below.

s(t)

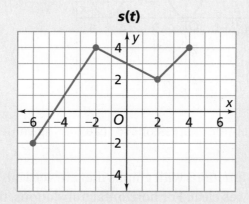

On the same coordinate grid, graph functions $p(t)$, $q(t)$, and $r(t)$ with these properties:

1. $p(t) = 3s(t)$ for all values of t.

2. $q(t) = 0.5s(t)$ for all values of t.

3. $r(t) = -s(t)$ for all values of t.

E Study the effects of changing constants in the algebraic expression for the linear function $f(x) = ax$. Do the same for the quadratic function $g(x) = bx^2$. Use a graphing calculator or a technology tool.

F Two functions are related by the equation $g(x) = kf(x)$ for all values of x. How are their graphs related?

A C E Homework starts on page 58.

3.3 Sliding Left and Right
Horizontal Translations of Functions

In Problem 3.1, you discovered how algebraic expressions are related if the graphs of those functions are related by translating vertically. There are similar connections between functions if their graphs are related by horizontal translations.

$f(x) = x^2$ and Two Translations

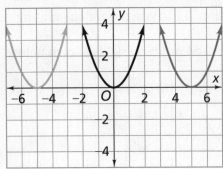

- How can you write algebraic expressions for calculating values of the other two functions?

The relationship between functions with graphs that are vertical translations of each other was clear. For horizontal translations, there is a different relationship between functions and graphs. See if you can determine a pattern as you work through the Problem.

Problem 3.3

A The functions with graphs shown above are translations of $f(x) = x^2$ with rules $g(x) = (x + 5)^2$ and $h(x) = (x - 5)^2$.

1. Which is the graph of $g(x)$? $h(x)$? Explain.

2. Sketch by hand graphs of $j(x) = (x + 3)^2$ and $k(x) = (x - 2.5)^2$. Explain how you know that your sketches are accurate. Test your thinking with a graphing calculator or online tool. Adjust your ideas as needed.

Problem **3.3** *continued*

B Use the diagram below.

1. Which graph represents the function $g(x) = f(x + 3)$ for all x? Explain.

2. Which graph represents the function $h(x) = f(x - 3)$ for all x? Explain.

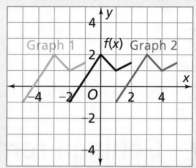

Two Horizontal Translations of Piecewise-Defined Function $f(x)$

C Think about your results for Questions A and B. Suppose you are given a graph of a function $f(x)$ and a positive number k. Explain what you could say about the shape and location of graphs for these related functions.

1. $g(x) = f(x - k)$ for all x.

2. $h(x) = f(x + k)$ for all x.

D 1. Match each graph with the function it represents. Do not use a graphing calculator or online graphing tool. Justify your reasoning.

$$f(x) = (x - 3)^2 - 1$$
$$g(x) = (x + 3)^2 - 4$$
$$h(x) = -(x + 2)^2 + 9$$
$$j(x) = -(x - 2)^2 + 4$$

Graphs of Four Functions

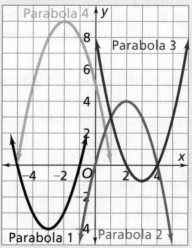

2. Explain the effects of changing a, b, and c in $f(x) = a(x - b)^2 + c$. Use a graphing calculator or online software to test the changes.

continued on the next page >

> **Problem 3.3** *continued*
>
> **E** If m and k are positive numbers, explain what you could say about the shape and location of graphs for these related functions.
>
>   **1.** $r(x) = f(x + k) + m$ for all x.   **2.** $s(x) = f(x - k) + m$ for all x.
>
>   **3.** $t(x) = f(x - k) - m$ for all x.   **4.** $u(x) = f(x + k) - m$ for all x.

A C E Homework starts on page 58.

3.4 Getting From Here to There
Transforming $y = x^2$

In Problems 3.1, 3.2, and 3.3 you discovered how changes in quadratic function rules lead to changes in their graphs. Suppose a, b, and c represent any positive numbers. You should be able to predict the shape and location for any graph in the forms:

- $f(x) = a(x + b)^2 + c$ • $g(x) = a(x + b)^2 - c$
- $h(x) = a(x - b)^2 + c$ • $j(x) = a(x - b)^2 - c$

Think back to your work in *Frogs, Fleas, and Painted Cubes*. In that Unit, you first solved problems involving quadratic expressions and graphs. You located the lines of symmetry and maximum or minimum points of those graphs.

Think more about the relationship between function rules and graphs for quadratic functions. The following Problem provides an opportunity to further develop and extend your understanding.

> **Problem 3.4**
>
> Answer the questions below. Check your ideas by graphing the function.
>
> **A** For each of these functions, find the line of symmetry. Identify the coordinates of the maximum or minimum point on its graph. Write down any patterns you notice.
>
>   **1.** $f(x) = x^2$ **2.** $g(x) = x^2 + 3$ **3.** $h(x) = x^2 - 5$
>
>   **4.** $f(x) = -x^2$ **5.** $g(x) = -x^2 + 3$ **6.** $h(x) = -x^2 - 5$

Problem **3.4** *continued*

B For each of these functions, find the line of symmetry. Identify the coordinates of the maximum or minimum point on its graph. Write down any patterns you notice.

1. $f(x) = (x - 4)^2$
2. $g(x) = (x + 3)^2$
3. $h(x) = (x - 4)^2 - 5$
4. $j(x) = (x + 3)^2 - 1$
5. $k(x) = -(x - 4)^2 - 5$
6. $h(x) = -(x + 3)^2 + 2$

C For each of these functions, find the line of symmetry. Identify the coordinates of the maximum or minimum point on its graph. Write down any patterns you notice.

1. $f(x) = 2x^2$
2. $g(x) = 4x^2 + 3$
3. $h(x) = -3x^2 - 5$
4. $j(x) = 0.5(x - 4)^2$
5. $k(x) = 2(x + 3)^2$
6. $m(x) = -3(x - 4)^2$
7. $j(x) = 0.5(x - 4)^2 + 2$
8. $k(x) = -2(x + 3)^2 - 1$
9. $m(x) = -3(x - 4)^2 - 5$

D Suppose a and b are non-negative numbers (i.e. $a \geq 0$ and $b \geq 0$). For parts (1)–(4), find the following:

- line of symmetry
- coordinates of the maximum or minimum point on the graph

1. $f(x) = a(x + b)^2 + c$
2. $f(x) = a(x - b)^2 + c$
3. $f(x) = -a(x + b)^2 + c$
4. $f(x) = -a(x - b)^2 + c$

Note on Notation The functions in parts (1)–(4) differ only by where the positive and negative signs are placed in their rules. The symbol $\pm$ can be used to express all four cases in a short form. The notation "± 5" means "+5 or −5". The notation "$\pm a$" means "the number a and its additive inverse." So, "$f(x) = \pm a(x \pm b)^2 + c$" indicates four different cases.

E The maximum or minimum point on the graph of a quadratic function is called the *vertex*. Why do you think $f(x) = a(x \pm b)^2 \pm c$ is called the *vertex form* of a quadratic function?

A C E Homework starts on page 58.

Applications

Exercises 1–9 refer to the graph of a function $f(x)$.
On copies of the graph, draw graphs of these functions.

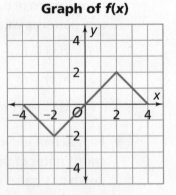

1. $g(x) = f(x) + 2$

2. $h(x) = f(x) - 1$

3. $j(x) = 0.5 f(x)$

4. $k(x) = 1.5 f(x)$

5. $m(x) = -2 f(x)$

6. $n(x) = f(x - 1)$

7. $p(x) = f(x + 0.5)$

8. $q(x) = -2 f(x) + 1$

9. $r(x) = f(x - 1) + 2$

10. Match each function with its graph. Explain how you made each match. Give coordinates of the maximum or minimum point on each graph. Be prepared to explain how you can find that information from just the function rule.

a. $a(x) = x^2$

b. $b(x) = (x - 2)^2$

c. $c(x) = -(x - 2)^2 - 2$

d. $d(x) = (x + 2)^2 - 2$

e. $e(x) = 0.5x^2$

f. $f(x) = 1.5x^2$

g. $g(x) = -(x - 3)^2$

h. $h(x) = -x^2 - 2$

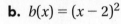

Parabolas 1 and 2

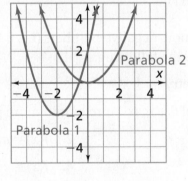

Parabolas 3 and 4

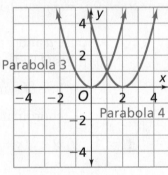

Parabolas 5 and 6

Parabolas 7 and 8

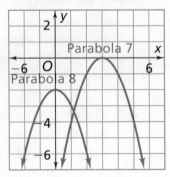

Connections

Exercises 11–15 refer to the following figure.

Five Transformations of a Flag

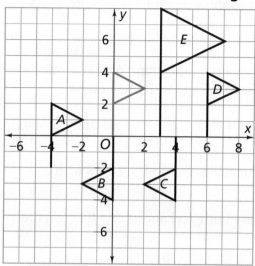

For each flag:

- Give the coordinate rule $(x, y) \rightarrow (\blacksquare, \blacksquare)$ for the transformation that maps the red flag to the given flag.
- Identify the kind of transformation(s) involved.

11. Flag A

12. Flag B

13. Flag C

14. Flag D

15. Flag E

Extensions

16. The function $f(x) = x^2 - 4x - 5$ can also be expressed as $f(x) = (x - 5)(x + 1)$ and $f(x) = (x - 2)^2 - 9$.

  a. Use algebraic reasoning to show that the three expressions are equivalent.

  b. Find the y-intercept, x-intercept(s), line of symmetry, and maximum or minimum point on the graph of $f(x)$. Explain which algebraic expression makes each calculation easiest.

17. a. Suppose $g(x) = f(2x)$ when $f(x) = x^2 - 4x - 5$. Find the standard expression for $g(x)$.

  Hint: Replace each occurrence of x in $x^2 - 4x - 5$ with $2x$. Simplify the result.

  b. Sketch a graph that shows both $f(x)$ and $g(x) = f(2x)$ on the same axes.

  c. Find the y-intercept, x-intercept(s), line of symmetry, and maximum or minimum point on the graph of $g(x)$.

  d. How does replacement of x with $2x$ seem to change the graph of $f(x)$? The properties of $f(x)$?

18. a. Suppose $g(x) = f(0.5x)$ when $f(x) = x^2 - 4x - 5$. Find the standard expression for $g(x)$.

  b. Sketch a graph that shows both $f(x)$ and $g(x) = f(0.5x)$ on the same axes.

  c. Find the y-intercept, x-intercept(s), line of symmetry, and maximum or minimum point on the graph of $g(x)$.

  d. How does replacement of x with $0.5x$ seem to change the graph of $f(x)$? The properties of $f(x)$?

19. Think about your work on Exercises 17–18. How do you think the graph of $g(x) = f(kx)$ is related to that of $f(x)$?

20. Test your conjecture in Exercise 19. Draw and compare graphs of these pairs of functions.

  a. $f(x) = x^2$ and $f(3x) = (3x)^2$

  b. $f(x) = x^2 - 1$ and $f(0.5x) = (0.5x)^2 - 1$

  c. $f(x) = x^2 - 6x$ and $f(2x) = 4x^2 - 12x$

In this Investigation, you studied the relationships between functions whose graphs are related by various familiar geometric transformations. These questions will help you summarize what you have learned.

Think about your answers. Discuss your ideas with other students and your teacher. Then write a summary of your findings in your notebook.

1. **How** will the rule for a function $f(x)$ change if the graph is:

   a. Translated up or down by k?

   b. Stretched away from or toward the x-axis by a factor of k?

   c. Translated left or right by k?

2. **How** does the vertex form of a quadratic equation like $f(x) = (x - h)^2 + k$ (where h and k are positive numbers) help to sketch the graph of the function?

Common Core Mathematical Practices

As you worked on the Problems in this Investigation, you used prior knowledge to make sense of them. You also applied Mathematical Practices to solve the Problems. Think back over your work, the ways you thought about the Problems, and how you used Mathematical Practices.

Shawna described her thoughts in the following way:

In Problem 3.3 we had trouble understanding why the graph of $f(x + 3)$ would be 3 units left of the graph of $f(x)$.

We looked at several examples, like $g(x) = (x + 1.5)^2$ and $h(x) = (x - 1.5)^2$. We could see that the graph of $g(x)$ would be 1.5 units left of $f(x) = x^2$, but we could not figure out why.

Eventually we figured out the meaning of the function rule $g(x) = f(x + 3)$. Each point on the graph of $g(x)$ is the same height as a corresponding point on the graph of $f(x)$. The graph of $f(x)$, however, is 3 units to the right. So the graph of $g(x)$ must be identical to that of $f(x)$, but 3 units to the left.

It might be easier to just memorize this, but it we wanted to understand why it worked.

Common Core Standards for Mathematical Practice

MP1 Make sense of problems and persevere in solving them.

 • What other Mathematical Practices can you identify in Shawna's reasoning?

• Describe a Mathematical Practice that you and your classmates used to solve a different Problem.

Solving Quadratic Equations Algebraically

In *Frogs, Fleas and Painted Cubes*, you learned to solve quadratic equations such as $(x - 2)(x - 1) = 0$. You also learned that you can write quadratic functions in different ways using equivalent expressions. Each equivalent form of the expression provides different information about the function.

Three Forms of Quadratic Functions

Form:	Standard	Factored	Vertex
Function	$f(x) = ax^2 + bx + c$	$g(x) = (x - m)(x - n)$	$h(x) = a(x - p)^2 + q$
Characteristics Revealed	y-intercept at $(0, c)$	zeros at $(m, 0)$ and $(n, 0)$	vertex at (p, q)
Example	$f(x) = 2x^2 + 4x + 1$ has y-intercept $(0, 1)$.	$g(x) = (x - 3)(x - 4)$ has zeros $(3, 0)$, $(4, 0)$.	$h(x) = (x - 3)^2 + 1$ has vertex $(3, 1)$.

$f(x) = 2x^2 + 4x + 1$ $g(x) = (x - 3)(x - 4)$ $h(x) = (x - 3)^2 + 1$

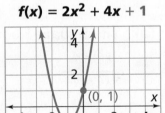
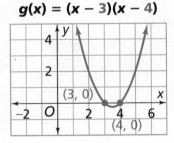
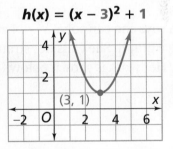

Common Core State Standards

A-SSE.B.3b Complete the square in a quadratic expression to reveal the maximum or minimum value of the function it defines.

A-REI.B.4b Solve quadratic equations by inspection, taking square roots, completing the square, the quadratic formula, and factoring, as appropriate to the initial form of the equation. Recognize when the quadratic formula gives complex solutions and write them as $a \pm bi$ for real numbers a and b.

Also A-REI.B.4, A-REI.B.4a, A-SSE.A.1b, A-SSE.B.3, F-IF.C.8a

You can use your knowledge of different quadratic forms to find more strategies for solving quadratic equations. Graphing is one possible strategy for solving.

$f(x) = x^2$ and $g(x) = (x - 3)^2$

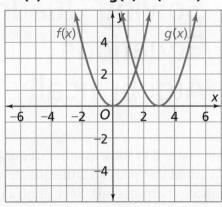

- If $f(x) = x^2$, how would you solve $x^2 = 4$ from the graph of $f(x)$?

- If $g(x) = (x - 3)^2$, how would you solve $(x - 3)^2 = 4$ from the graph of $g(x)$?

- What points on $f(x)$ and $g(x)$ correspond to your solutions?

- How are these points related?

4.1 Applying Square Roots

Anita says she can solve $x^2 = 4$ and $(x - 3)^2 = 4$ without using a graph. She calls her strategy, *Take the Square Root*. Her work is shown below.

> **Take the Square Root**
> $x^2 = 4$
> $\sqrt{x^2} = \sqrt{4}$
> $x = 2$

Tawanda says she can amend Anita's strategy so it finds both solutions for $x^2 = 4$.

> **Amended Strategy**
> $x^2 = 4$
> $\sqrt{x^2} = \pm\sqrt{4}$
> $x = \sqrt{4}$ or $x = -\sqrt{4}$
> $x = 2$ or $x = -2$

Tawanda is using one of the *properties of equality*. The property states that you can take the square root of both sides of an equation. If you do, then the new equation formed has the same solutions as the original equation.

- Using Tawanda's amended strategy, what are the algebraic solutions for $(x - 3)^2 = 4$?

- How do these algebraic solutions compare to the graphical solutions for $(x - 3)^2 = 4$?

- Can you use Anita's amended *Take the Square Root* strategy to solve any quadratic equation?

As you use algebraic and graphing strategies to solve quadratic equations, look for connections among your strategies.

Problem 4.1

A **1.** Use a symbolic method to solve these equations.

  a. $(x + 1)^2 = 9$ **b.** $(x - 3)^2 = 0.25$ **c.** $(x + 0.5)^2 = 4$

2. a. Graph $h(x) = (x + 1)^2$ using a graphing tool. Where on the graph do you look for the solutions for $(x + 1)^2 = 9$? What are the solutions?

  b. Graph $j(x) = (x + 1)^2 - 9$ using a graphing tool. Where on the graph do you look for the solutions for $(x + 1)^2 - 9 = 0$? Give the solutions.

  c. How are the graphical solutions for $(x + 1)^2 = 9$ and $(x + 1)^2 - 9 = 0$ related to each other?

3. Solve symbolically. Then check your solutions graphically. In each case, explain how your solutions relate to the line of symmetry.

  a. $(x - 3)^2 - 4 = 0$ **b.** $(x - 3)^2 - 2 = 0$

B Kailey says she could have solved $(x + 1)^2 = 9$ without graphing or taking square roots. She calls her method a *Factoring Strategy*.

> **Factoring Strategy**
>
> $(x + 1)^2 = 9$
> $(x + 1)(x + 1) = 9$
> $x^2 + 2x + 1 = 9$
> $x^2 + 2x - 8 = 0$
> $(x + 4)(x - 2) = 0$

How does Kailey finish her method? Do her solutions agree with your answer to Question A, part (1)?

continued on the next page >

Problem 4.1 *continued*

C Use Kailey's method or Anita's method to solve these quadratic equations. If neither strategy works, explain why.

1. $(x + 4)^2 = 25$ **2.** $(x - 4)^2 = 5$

3. $x^2 + 8x - 9 = 0$ **4.** $x^2 + 8x + 7 = 0$

5. $x^2 - 6x + 9 = 0$ **6.** $(x + 2)^2 = 2$

7. $x^2 + 4x + 4 = 2$ **8.** $x^2 + 4x = 4$

D When does Kailey's factoring method work? When does Anita's square root method work? When does graphing work?

A C E Homework starts on page 76.

4.2 Completing the Square

In Problem 4.1, you were able to solve many different quadratic equations. Some equations, however, cannot be solved using the symbolic methods discussed in Problem 4.1. Consider the quadratic equation below.

$$x^2 + 4x = 4 \text{ or } x^2 + 4x - 4 = 0$$

- Suppose $f(x) = x^2 + 4x - 4$. What do we know about the graph of this function?

Suppose you could write this function in vertex form. Then you would know more about the graph of this function. Start by plotting some points and drawing a graph. You can then determine the vertex form from the graph you drew.

$f(x) = x^2 + 4x - 4$

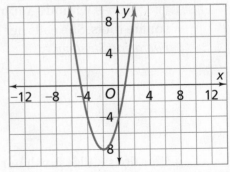

- Explain how you can tell the vertex form of the function is $f(x) = (x + 2)^2 - 8$ from the graph.

- How can you use the graph to find the solutions for $(x + 2)^2 - 8 = 0$?

From the vertex form of the equation you can find solutions for $(x + 2)^2 - 8 = 0$ symbolically.

$$(x + 2)^2 = 8$$
$$\sqrt{(x + 2)^2} = \pm\sqrt{8}$$
$$(x + 2) = \sqrt{8} \quad \text{or} \quad (x + 2) = -\sqrt{8}$$
$$x = -2 + \sqrt{8} \quad \text{or} \quad x = -2 - \sqrt{8}$$

- How are these solutions like or unlike the solutions you found graphically?

- How are these solutions related to the line of symmetry of the graph of $f(x)$?

- How can we take any quadratic equation, like $x^2 + 4x - 4 = 0$, and rewrite it in a vertex form?

There is a way to write any quadratic equation in a vertex form. The key is to recognize the pattern for the expanded form of a perfect square like $(x + 2)^2$.

Problem 4.2

A In parts (1) and (2), look for patterns that help you recognize perfect square quadratic expressions.

1. Write each expression in equivalent standard form, $ax^2 + bx + c$.

   a. $(x + 1)^2$ **b.** $(x - 3)^2$ **c.** $(x + 6)^2$ **d.** $(x - 0.2)^2$

2. Write each of these expressions in equivalent factored form.

   a. $x^2 + 8x + 16$ **b.** $x^2 + 6x + 9$

   c. $x^2 - 18x + 81$ **d.** $x^2 - 10x + 25$

3. **a.** What value of c would make $x^2 + 12x + c$ a perfect square? Explain your reasoning.

   b. What value of b would make $x^2 + bx + 49$ a perfect square? Explain your reasoning.

B Brendan can use the pattern for $(x + a)^2$ to rewrite any quadratic expression in vertex form. Then he uses the vertex form to solve any quadratic equation. For example, he wants to solve $x^2 + 4x + 3 = 0$. His work is shown below.

> $x^2 + 4x + 3 = 0$
> "$x^2 + 4x$" looks like the beginning of the perfect square $x^2 + 4x + 4$.
> $x^2 + 4x + 4 - 4 + 3 = 0$

1. Is this still equivalent to $x^2 + 4x + 3 = 0$? Explain.

2. Next he writes
> $(x^2 + 4x + 4) - 4 + 3 = 0$
> $(x + 2)^2 - 1 = 0$

   Where did the "-1" come from?

3. How would you finish Brendan's method?

Problem 4.2 *continued*

C Try Brendan's method on the following quadratic equations.

1. $x^2 + 6x + 5 = 0$ **2.** $x^2 - 8x + 11 = 0$

3. $x^2 + 4x - 4 = 0$ **4.** $x^2 - 6x - 1 = 0$

D Brendan's method for rewriting $x^2 + 4x + 3 = 0$ involves adding a 4 and subtracting a 4 on the left side of the equation. He ends up with $(x + 2)^2 - 1$ in place of $x^2 + 4x - 3$. The diagram shows a square with sides $(x + 2)$ and area $(x + 2)^2$.

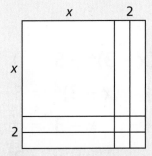

1. a. On a copy of the square, locate $(x + 2)^2 - 1$ in the picture. Shade this in one color.

     b. Explain how this picture shows that $x^2 + 4x + 3$ and $(x + 2)^2 - 1$ are equivalent.

2. Make a sketch that shows that $(x + 3)^2 - 2$ and $x^2 + 6x + 7$ are equivalent.

3. Use the sketch below to find an equivalent expression for $x^2 + 8x + 3$.

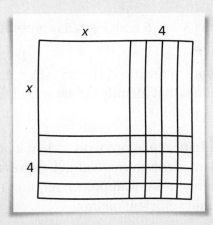

4. Draw a square that will help you find an equivalent expression in vertex form for $x^2 + 6x + 8$.

5. Consider the standard form for quadratic expressions, $x^2 + bx + c$. Is it always possible to find an equivalent expression in vertex form? Explain.

6. How does completing the square in a quadratic expression reveal the maximum or minimum value of the related quadratic function?

A C E Homework starts on page 76.

4.3 The Quadratic Formula

The quadratic equation $x^2 - 6x + 4 = 0$ can be written in equivalent vertex form as $(x - 3)^2 - 5 = 0$. This leads to a solution of the equation symbolically and graphically.

$$(x - 3)^2 - 5 = 0$$
$$(x - 3)^2 = 5$$
$$x - 3 = \pm\sqrt{5}$$
$$x = 3\pm\sqrt{5}$$
$$x \approx 5.24 \text{ or}$$
$$x \approx 0.76$$

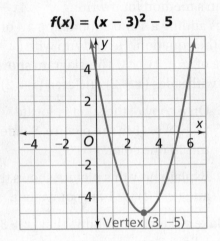

$f(x) = (x - 3)^2 - 5$

Vertex (3, −5)

- Why are $x = 5.24$ and $x = 0.76$ approximate solutions for $x^2 - 6x + 4 = 0$?

- How are the exact solutions $3 + \sqrt{5}$ and $3 - \sqrt{5}$ represented on the graph?

- You can complete the square to rewrite $f(x) = x^2 - 6x + 4$ as $f(x) = (x - 3)^2 - 5$. How does that identify the zeros and the maximum or minimum point of the function?

This approach to solving quadratic equations works when it only takes a few steps to find the vertex form of the given quadratic expression. There are many cases, however, where this same approach requires many more steps. Let us now consider a more efficient method.

Completing the square is more complicated when the coefficient of the x^2 is not 1. Consider $3x^2 + 5x + 1 = 0$.

Mathematicians have developed a general formula to solve quadratic equations. This formula is called the **Quadratic Formula.** This formula calculates the solutions to any quadratic equation in the form $ax^2 + bx + c = 0$ when $a \neq 0$. The formula says solutions will be:

$$x = \frac{-b}{2a} + \frac{\sqrt{b^2 - 4ac}}{2a} \text{ and } x = \frac{-b}{2a} - \frac{\sqrt{b^2 - 4ac}}{2a}$$

The Quadratic Formula may look like a complicated procedure for solving equations. It is only a matter of matching and substituting the coefficients. Then you perform the arithmetic using the Order of Operations.

- Explain how the formula gives these solutions to the equation $3x^2 + 5x + 1 = 0$.

$$x = \frac{-5}{6} + \frac{\sqrt{13}}{6} \text{ and } x = \frac{-5}{6} - \frac{\sqrt{13}}{6}.$$

Problem 4.3

Ⓐ In parts (1)–(6), use the Quadratic Formula to solve these quadratic equations.

1. $2x^2 + 9x + 6 = 0$

2. $4x^2 + 3x - 5 = 0$

3. $-3x^2 + 5x + 1 = 0$

4. $-2x^2 + 7x - 6 = 0$

5. $12 + 18x + 4x^2 = 0$

6. $-3x + 4x^2 - 5 = 0$

continued on the next page >

Problem **4.3**　*continued*

B You can also use **completing the square** to solve all of the equations in Question A. However, this process would take many steps. You can use completing the square to develop the Quadratic Formula. This formula can be used to solve any quadratic equation. To see why the formula works, Kalvin starts with an example.

1. Kalvin begins to solve $2x^2 + 9x + 6 = 0$ by completing the square. His work is shown below.

$$2x^2 + 9x + 6 = 0$$

$$2\left(x^2 + \frac{9}{2}x + 3\right) = 0 \quad \text{Factor 2 out of each term on the left.}$$

$$x^2 + \frac{9}{2}x + 3 = 0$$

Need to write above equation in vertex form.

$$x^2 + \frac{9}{2}x + \left(\frac{9}{4}\right)^2 - \left(\frac{9}{4}\right)^2 + 3 = 0$$

Complete this to find solutions for x.

2. Follow the same logic Kalvin used in part (1). Complete the reasoning on both sides of the table. Provide reasons for each step.

Developing the Quadratic Formula

$2x^2 + 9x + 6 = 0$	$ax^2 + bx + c = 0$	Reasons
$2\left(x^2 + \left(\frac{9}{2}\right)x + 3\right) = 0$	$a\left(x^2 + \left(\frac{b}{a}\right)x + \frac{c}{a}\right) = 0$	■
$x^2 + \left(\frac{9}{2}\right)x + 3 = 0$	$x^2 + \left(\frac{b}{a}\right)x + \frac{c}{a} = 0$	■
$x^2 + \left(\frac{9}{2}\right)x + \left(\frac{9}{4}\right)^2 - \left(\frac{9}{4}\right)^2 + 3 = 0$	$x^2 + \left(\frac{b}{a}\right)x + \left(\frac{b}{2a}\right)^2 - \left(\frac{b}{2a}\right)^2 + \frac{c}{a} = 0$	■
$\left(x + \frac{9}{4}\right)^2 - \frac{33}{16} = 0$	$(x + ■)^2 - ■ = 0$	■
■	■	■
■	■	■
$x = ■$ or $x = ■$	$x = ■$ or $x = ■$	■

Problem 4.3 *continued*

C Choose a different strategy to solve each of these quadratic equations, if possible.

1. $(x - 4)^2 - 9 = 0$ **2.** $2x^2 + 5x - 2 = 0$

3. $x^2 + 1 = 0$ **4.** $x^2 - 8x - 9 = 0$

A C E Homework starts on page 76.

4.4 Complex Numbers

· ·

The Quadratic Formula gives an algorithm for solving any quadratic equation in the form $ax^2 + bx + c = 0$. Sometimes you get strange results when using the formula. Consider the equation $x^2 + 4x + 5 = 0$. According to the Quadratic Formula, the solutions to that equation should be

$$x = -2 + \frac{\sqrt{-4}}{2} \text{ and } x = -2 - \frac{\sqrt{-4}}{2}.$$

The solutions require the square roots of negative numbers. What is that number? Is it a real number?

The graph of $f(x) = x^2 + 4x + 5$ shows the problem from another view.

f(x) = x² + 4x + 5

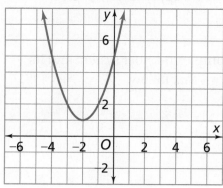

The seemingly impossible calculation required to solve $x^2 + 4x + 5 = 0$ puzzled mathematicians for thousands of years. Eventually, they decided to extend the number system. The extended number system includes the real numbers and numbers like $\sqrt{-1}$. The process began with defining a solution to the equation $x^2 + 1 = 0$.

If $x^2 + 1 = 0$, then $x^2 = -1$.

So $x = \pm\sqrt{-1}$.

In order to have a solution, we need to define a new number. This number requires the property that its square is equal to -1. We write it as the imaginary number i, where $i = \sqrt{-1}$.

All previous mathematics had suggested the impossibility of such a number. The table below shows some numbers that result from the extension of the number system.

Real Numbers	Imaginary Numbers	Complex Numbers
3, $\sqrt{5}$, $\frac{\pi}{3}$, 2.7, $\frac{4}{9}$, $-\sqrt{7}$, $0.\overline{3}$ $a + bi$ $(b = 0)$	$i = \sqrt{-1}$ $7i$, $-i\sqrt{2}$, $6i + 7i$ $a + bi$ $(a = 0)$	7, $8 + 3i$, $2 - 3i$, $0.\overline{3}$, $\frac{\pi}{3}$, $-6i$, $\sqrt{3} + 2i$ $a + bi$

The set of real numbers and the **imaginary numbers** is called the set of **complex numbers.**

 Do the operations for real numbers apply to complex numbers?

You will get some ideas about the complex number system and its operations by answering the questions that follow.

Problem 4.4

(A) In this Question, you will use the fact that $\sqrt{-1} = i$.

   1. Explain why $(2i)^2 = -4$, so $2i$ is a square root of -4.

   2. Explain why $(-3i)^2 = -9$, so $-3i$ is a square root of -9.

   3. Use i to write $\sqrt{-49}$ as a complex number.

   4. Use i to write $\sqrt{-\frac{4}{9}}$ as a complex number.

(B) **1.** Explain why it makes sense that $7i + 11i = 18i$ and, in general, $bi + di = (b + d)i$.

   2. Write the sum $(5 + 3i) + (6 + 4i)$ as a number in the form $a + bi$.

   3. Write the difference $(5 + 3i) - (6 + 4i)$ as a number in the form $a + bi$.

(C) Apply what you know about multiplying binomials and the imaginary number i to find each product. Write these products as a complex number in the form $a + bi$.

   1. $(5 + 3i)(6 + 4i)$

   2. $(5 - 3i)(6 + 4i)$

   3. $(5 + 3i)^2$

(D) Use the Quadratic Formula to solve these equations. Write your answers as complex numbers in the form $a + bi$.

   1. $x^2 + 2x + 2 = 0$

   2. $x^2 - 4x + 13 = 0$

   3. $-x^2 + 8x - 17 = 0$

   4. $x^2 + 6x + 11 = 0$

(E) For each equation from Question D, graph the corresponding quadratic function. Explain how you can tell from the graph of a quadratic function whether the related equation will have real or imaginary solutions.

(A)(C)(E) Homework starts on page 76.

Applications

1. Solve for x.

   a. $(x - 3)^2 - 1 = 0$

   b. $(x + 1)^2 - 4 = 0$

   c. $(x - 1)^2 - 3 = 0$

   d. $(x + 1)^2 - 1 = 0$

   e. $4(x + 1)^2 - 4 = 0$

   f. $4(x - 1)^2 - 3 = 0$

2. The functions below correspond to the equations you solved in Exercise 1. Use information about the vertex form and the zeroes you found in Exercise 1. Match each function to the correct graph. Explain your thinking in each case.

   a. $a(x) = (x - 3)^2 - 1$

   b. $b(x) = (x + 1)^2 - 4$

   c. $c(x) = (x - 1)^2 - 3$

   d. $d(x) = (x + 1)^2 - 1$

   e. $e(x) = 4(x + 1)^2 - 4$

   f. $f(x) = 4(x - 1)^2 - 3$

   Parabola 1

   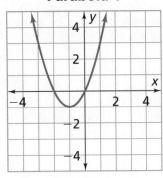

   Parabola 2

   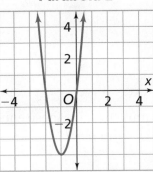

   Parabola 3

   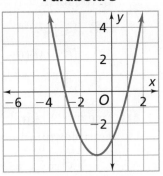

   Parabola 4

   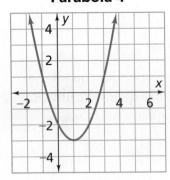

   Parabola 5

   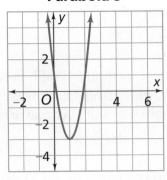

   Parabola 6

   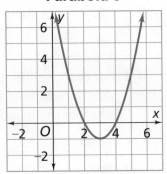

In Exercises 3–8, expand each expression to give a perfect square trinomial.

3. $(x + 7)^2$

4. $(x - 7)^2$

5. $(2x + 7)^2$

6. $(2x - 7)^2$

7. $(x + p)^2$

8. $\left(x + \dfrac{q}{s}\right)^2$

For Exercises 9–14, each quadratic function is in standard form.

- Complete the square to write each function in vertex form.
- Identify coordinates of the maximum or minimum point.
- Identify the x-intercept(s) and y-intercept.
- State which form is more convenient to identify coordinates of the maximum/minimum point, x-intercept(s), and y-intercept.

9. $f(x) = x^2 + 2x - 3$

10. $g(x) = x^2 - 4x - 5$

11. $h(x) = x^2 - 6x + 5$

12. $j(x) = x^2 + 4x + 2$

13. $k(x) = -x^2 + 3x - 1$

14. $l(x) = -x^2 + 8x - 5$

For Exercises 15–20, use the Quadratic Formula to solve the equations. Give both the exact result provided by the formula and a decimal approximation, where appropriate.

15. $5x^2 + 10x - 15 = 0$

16. $3x^2 + 2x - 7 = 0$

17. $-4x^2 + 5x - 1 = 0$

18. $7x + 3x^2 = -3$

19. $0 = 2 + 3x + x^2$

20. $3x^2 - 2 = 6x$

21. Solve the equation $x^2 - 6x + 13 = 0$. Write the solutions as complex numbers in the form $a + bi$ and $a - bi$ if needed.

Write the result of the indicated sum, difference, or product in the form of a single complex number $a + bi$.

22. $(3 + 7i) + (13 - 4i)$

23. $(3 + 7i) - (13 - 4i)$

24. $(3 + 7i)(13 - 4i)$

25. $(3 + 7i)(3 - 7i)$

Connections

26. Bianca's teacher asks her students to find a quadratic function that has zeroes at $(-2, 0)$ and $(0, 0)$.

a. Bianca says that there is only one quadratic function that fits this description. She makes the following table of values for her function. Is $f(x)$ a quadratic function? Explain.

x	-2	-1	0	1	2	3
$f(x)$	0	-1	0	3	8	15

b. Aleshanee says she can make a different table and different graph, with the same zeroes. Is $g(x)$ a quadratic function? Explain.

x	-2	-1	0	1	2	3
$g(x)$	0	-4	0	12	32	60

c. How are $f(x)$ and $g(x)$ related to each other?

27. Write expressions in vertex form, $a(x - b)^2 + c$, for functions with these properties.

a. minimum point at $(3, -5)$

b. maximum point at $(1, 4)$

c. minimum point at $(-3, 1)$

d. maximum point at $(-5, -2)$

28. Write equations that have these properties.

a. solutions are whole numbers

b. solutions are integers, but not whole numbers

c. solutions are real numbers, but not rational numbers

d. solutions are complex numbers, but not real numbers

29. In each pair of calculations, write the two results in simplest possible equivalent form. Explain how the reasoning in each case is based on number system properties.

   a. $(3 + 2i) + (7 - 3i)$ and $(3 + 2x) + (7 - 3x)$

   b. $(3 + 2i) - (7 - 3i)$ and $(3 + 2x) - (7 - 3x)$

   c. $(3 + 2i)(7 - 3i)$ and $(3 + 2x)(7 - 3x)$

   d. $-(7 - 3i)$ and $-(7 - 3x)$

Did You Know?

In 1806, J. R. Argand developed a method for displaying complex numbers graphically. Any complex number could be displayed as a point in the coordinate plane. His method, called the *Argand Diagram*, relates the *x*-axis (real axis) with the *y*-axis (imaginary axis).
The *x*-values are real numbers *a*.
The *y*-values are imaginary numbers *bi*.

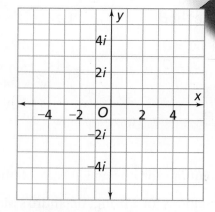

30. On a copy of the coordinate plane shown above, label each point with the complex number it represents.

   a. $3 + 2i$ **b.** $4 - 3i$ **c.** $-2 + 4i$ **d.** $-4 - 3i$

31. Name the geometric transformations that map points representing any complex number as indicated.

   a. $(3 + 2i) \rightarrow (3 - 2i)$ and, in general, $(a + bi) \rightarrow (a - bi)$

   b. $(3 + 2i) \rightarrow (-3 + 2i)$ and, in general, $(a + bi) \rightarrow (-a + bi)$

   c. $(3 + 2i) \rightarrow (-3 - 2i)$ and, in general, $(a + bi) \rightarrow (-a - bi)$

   d. $(3 + 2i) \rightarrow (7 + 5i)$ and, in general, $(a + bi) \rightarrow (a + 4) + (b + 3)i$

Extensions

32. The following tables each show a quadratic relationship.

x	−2	−1	0	1	2	3
f(x)	0	−1	0	3	8	15

x	−2	−1	0	1	2	3
g(x)	0	−2	0	6	16	30

   a. For each table, find the function that represents the table.

   b. How are the functions related to each other?

33. Alejandro and Latasia are solving the equation $4x^2 + 32x + 60 = 0$. Their methods are shown below.

> **Alejandro's Method**
> $4x^2 + 32x + 60 = 0$
> $(2x + 10)(2x + 6) = 0$
>
>
>
> **Latasia's Method**
> $4x^2 + 32x + 60 = 0$
> $4(x^2 + 8x + 15) = 0$
> $x^2 + 8x + 15 = 0$
> $(x + 5)(x + 3) = 0$

   a. What are the solutions for x using Latasia's Method?

   b. What are the solutions for x using Alejandro's Method?

   c. Which of the two methods is correct (*Latasia's, Alejandro's, both, or neither*)?

34. Hai and Jenna were asked to use the *completing the square* strategy to solve the equation $4x^2 + 16x - 48 = 0$.

Hai's Method

First, factor 4 from the left side to get
$$4(x^2 + 4x - 12) = 0$$

Then, solve $x^2 + 4x - 12 = 0$ like this:
$$x^2 + 4x + \blacksquare = 12$$
$$x^2 + 4x + 4 = 16$$
$$(x + 2)^2 = 16$$
$$x + 2 = 4 \text{ or } x + 2 = -4$$
$$x = -2 \text{ or } x = -6$$

OR

Jenna's Method

$$4x^2 + 16x + \blacksquare = 48$$
$$4x^2 + 16x + 64 = 48 + 64$$
$$(2x + 8)^2 = 112$$
$$2x + 8 = \pm\sqrt{112}$$
$$2x = -8 \pm\sqrt{112}$$
$$x = \frac{-8 \pm\sqrt{112}}{2}$$

Which of these two methods is correct? Explain.

35. a. You can use ideas from the Quadratic Formula proof to complete the square. These ideas cover all cases where the coefficient of x^2 is a number other than 1. Explain why each step in the process below is justified.

Step 1 $ax^2 + bx + c = a\left(x^2 + \frac{b}{a}x\right) + c$

Step 2 $\qquad\qquad = a\left(x^2 + \frac{b}{a}x + \left(\frac{b}{2a}\right)^2 - \left(\frac{b}{2a}\right)^2\right) + c$

Step 3 $\qquad\qquad = a\left(x^2 + \frac{b}{a}x + \frac{b^2}{4a^2} - \frac{b^2}{4a^2}\right) + c$

Step 4 $\qquad\qquad = a\left(x^2 + \frac{b}{a}x + \frac{b^2}{4a^2}\right) + \left(c - \frac{b^2}{4a}\right)$

Step 5 $\qquad\qquad = a\left(x + \frac{b}{2a}\right)^2 + \left(c - \frac{b^2}{4a}\right)$

b. Follow each step in the process demonstrated above to complete the square for the expression $2x^2 + 6x + 5$.

36. Use Step 5 in the process demonstrated in Exercise 35 to write each quadratic expression in equivalent vertex form.

a. $3x^2 + 5x + 7$ **b.** $-3x^2 + 5x - 7$ **c.** $6x^2 - 5x + 4$

37. For any complex number $a + bi$, the number $a - bi$ is called its **complex conjugate**. Show that the product of a complex number and its complex conjugate is always a real number. Simplify each expression below.

   a. $(3 + 2i)(3 - 2i)$ **b.** $(-3 - 2i)(-3 + 2i)$ **c.** $(a + bi)(a - bi)$

38. The relationship of each complex number to its complex conjugate can be used to define division of complex numbers.

   a. Explain why each step in this calculation of $(3 + 4i) \div (1 + 2i)$ makes sense.

      Step 1 $\dfrac{3 + 4i}{1 + 2i} = \dfrac{3 + 4i}{1 + 2i} \cdot \dfrac{1 - 2i}{1 - 2i}$

      Step 2 $= \dfrac{(3 + 4i)(1 - 2i)}{(1 + 2i)(1 - 2i)}$

      Step 3 $= \dfrac{11 - 2i}{5}$

      Step 4 $= \dfrac{11}{5} - \dfrac{2}{5}i$

   b. Write $(3 + 4i) \div (1 - 2i)$ in standard complex number form $a + bi$.

   c. Write $(3 - 4i) \div (1 + 2i)$ in standard complex number form $a + bi$.

39. Xavier applied what he knew about adding fractions to problems with variables in the denominator. For example, Xavier recalled that when adding $\frac{2}{3} + \frac{1}{5}$, the common denominator is $15 = 3 \cdot 5$. He used this strategy to find the sum $\frac{2}{3} + \frac{1}{a}$.

      Step 1 $\frac{2}{3} + \frac{1}{a} = \left(\frac{a}{a} \cdot \frac{2}{3}\right) + \left(\frac{3}{3} \cdot \frac{1}{a}\right)$

      Step 2 $= \frac{2a}{3a} + \frac{3}{3a}$

      Step 3 $= \frac{2a + 3}{3a}$

   Is Xavier's method correct? Explain.

40. Use a strategy similar to Exercise 39 to write each sum as a single fraction.

   a. $\dfrac{5}{b} + \dfrac{2}{5}$ **b.** $\dfrac{3}{d} + \dfrac{2}{c}$ **c.** $\dfrac{1}{a} + \dfrac{1}{4a^2}$

In this Investigation, you used algebraic reasoning to write quadratic expressions in equivalent vertex form. You developed the Quadratic Formula for solving quadratic equations. You also developed basic ideas about complex numbers. These questions will help you summarize what you have learned.

Think about your answers. Discuss your ideas with other students and your teacher. Then write a summary of your findings in your notebook.

1. **What** are the key steps in writing a quadratic expression like $x^2 + 6x + 11$ in vertex form?

2. **How** does the Quadratic Formula help to solve equations in the form $ax^2 + bx + c = 0$?

3. **What** methods do you have for solving quadratic equations, other than the Quadratic Formula?

4. **What** are the complex numbers? **How** are they added, subtracted, and multiplied?

Common Core Mathematical Practices

As you worked on the Problems in this Investigation, you used prior knowledge to make sense of them. You also applied Mathematical Practices to solve the Problems. Think back over your work, the ways you thought about the Problems, and how you used Mathematical Practices.

Hector described his thoughts in the following way:

We could solve quadratic equations like $(x - a)^2 = b$, by taking square roots of both sides. There are two solutions, $x = a + \sqrt{b}$ and $x = a - \sqrt{b}$. That was only useful for solving some quadratic equations.

We soon found out how to write any quadratic equation in this form. This process is called completing the square.

Once we understood the pattern of steps, we could do this every time. The steps are not difficult, but there are several of them.

We were glad that there was a formula that captured all of the steps at once.

....

Common Core Standards for Mathematical Practice
MP7 Look for and make use of structure.

- What other Mathematical Practices can you identify in Hector's reasoning?

- Describe a Mathematical Practice that you and your classmates used to solve a different Problem in this Investigation.

Polynomial Expressions, Functions, and Equations

Linear and quadratic functions, equations, and graphs are very familiar mathematical models. Situations occur when these functions are not good models for patterns in data. Consider the graph below.

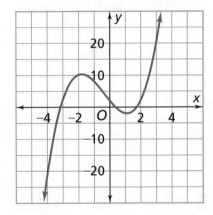

We cannot fit a linear, quadratic, exponential, or inverse variation function to model its shape.

You can produce graphs with more "hills" and "valleys" than quadratic graphs. You can extend those functions to include terms involving x^3, x^4, and even higher powers. For example, the function with graph shown above is $f(x) = x^3 + x^2 - 6x + 2$. The algebraic expression $x^3 + x^2 - 6x + 2$ is called a *polynomial*.

Common Core State Standards

A-APR.A.1 Understand that polynomials form a system analogous to the integers, namely, they are closed under the operations of addition, subtraction, and multiplication; add, subtract, and multiply polynomials.

F-IF.B.4. For a function that models a relationship between two quantities, interpret key features of graphs and tables in terms of the quantities, and sketch graphs showing key features given a verbal description of the relationship.

F-BF.A.1b. Combine standard function types using arithmetic operations.

Also F-IF.C.7a, F-IF.C.8a, F-IF.C.9

In general, a **polynomial** expression has the following form.

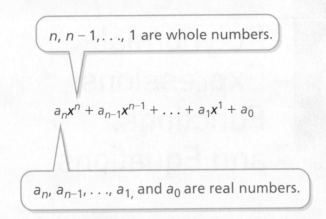

n, n − 1, . . ., 1 are whole numbers.

$$a_n x^n + a_{n-1}x^{n-1} + \ldots + a_1 x^1 + a_0$$

$a_n, a_{n-1}, \ldots, a_1,$ and a_0 are real numbers.

In the polynomial expression $x^3 + x^2 - 6x + 2$, the value of n is 3 and the coefficients are $a_3 = 1$, $a_2 = 1$, $a_1 = -6$, and $a_0 = 2$.

In the polynomial expression $5x^4 - 3x^2 + 4x - 7$, the value of n is 4 and the coefficients are $a_4 = 5$, $a_3 = 0$, $a_2 = -3$, $a_1 = 4$, and $a_0 = -7$.

A **polynomial function** is a function with a rule given by a polynomial expression.

The Problems of this Investigation will develop your understanding and skill in operating with polynomials. You will also graph polynomial functions and solve polynomial equations.

5.1 Properties of Polynomial Expressions and Functions

One of the most important characteristics of any polynomial expression is its degree. The **degree of a polynomial** is the greatest exponent of the variable that occurs in the expression. For example, a quadratic polynomial has degree 2. A polynomial with degree 3 is called a cubic polynomial. A polynomial with degree 4 is called a quartic polynomial.

Knowing the degree of a polynomial helps in predicting the shape of its graph. The degree of a polynomial also predicts solutions of related equations. Examine the graph of $f(x) = x^3 + x^2 - 6x + 2$ below.

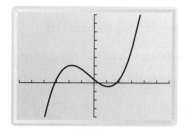
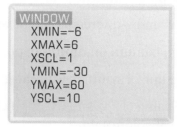

WINDOW
XMIN=-6
XMAX=6
XSCL=1
YMIN=-30
YMAX=60
YSCL=10

- How does the graph help you estimate solutions of the equation $x^3 + x^2 - 6x + 2 = 0$?

- How does the graph help you to identify intervals on which values of the function $f(x) = x^3 + x^2 - 6x + 2$ are increasing or decreasing?

- How does the graph help you to identify *local maximum* or *local minimum* points?

A calculator or computer graphing tool is useful in exploring properties of polynomial functions. You can see how changes in a polynomial lead to changes in the graph.

The zeros of a function tell you the x-intercepts of the graph. You can find the zeros for a function $p(x)$ by solving the equation $p(x) = 0$.

Problem 5.1

A For each of the following quadratic functions,

- Sketch a graph.

- Estimate or find exact coordinates of the maximum or minimum point.

- Identify intervals on the x-axis where function values are increasing and where function values are decreasing.

- Estimate or find exact coordinates for the x- and y-intercepts.

- Give the equation of the line of symmetry of the graph.

1. $f(x) = (x + 3)^2$
2. $g(x) = -x^2 + 3x + 4$
3. $h(x) = (x - 3)^2 - 9$
4. $j(x) = -x^2 + 5x - 6$

continued on the next page >

Problem 5.1 *continued*

B For any quadratic polynomial function:

1. How many x- and y-intercepts can be expected for the graph?

2. How many maximum or minimum points can occur on the graph?

3. Where is the line of symmetry for the graph located?

4. How do the value of $f(x)$ and its graph change as the value of x grows very large in absolute value?

C For each of the following cubic polynomial functions,

- Sketch a graph.

- Estimate coordinates of the local maximum or minimum points.

- Identify intervals on the x-axis where function values are increasing and where function values are decreasing.

- Estimate coordinates for the x- and y-intercepts.

- Give the equation for any line of symmetry of the graph.

1. $f(x) = x^3 + x^2 - 2x - 3$
2. $g(x) = -x^3 + x^2 - 2x - 3$
3. $h(x) = -x^3 - x^2 + 2x$
4. $j(x) = x^3$

D Use your graphing tool to explore other cubic polynomials. Then make conjectures about answers to the following questions about any such function.

1. How many x- and y-intercepts can be expected for the graph?

2. How many local maximum or minimum points can occur on the graph?

3. How many lines of symmetry does the graph have? Where are these lines located?

4. How do the value of $f(x)$ and its graph change as the value of x grows very large in absolute value?

Problem **5.1** *continued*

E Think about your work with linear, quadratic, and cubic polynomials. Make conjectures about answers to the following questions about quartic polynomial functions. Quartic polynomials are rules in the form $f(x) = a_4x^4 + a_3x^3 + a_2x^2 + a_1x + a_0$. Test your ideas by graphing a variety of examples of such functions.

1. How many x- and y-intercepts would you expect for the graph?

2. How many maximum or minimum points can occur on the graph?

3. How many lines of symmetry are there for the graph?

4. How do the value of $f(x)$ and its graph change as the value of x grows very large in absolute value?

F The degree of any polynomial tells instantly some important information about its graph.

1. What common symmetry do you see in the graphs of $f(x) = x^2$, $g(x) = x^4$, and $h(x) = x^6$?

2. What common symmetry do you see in the graphs of $j(x) = x$, $k(x) = x^3$, and $m(x) = x^5$?

3. Any function for which $f(x) = f(-x)$ for all x is called an even function.

   a. Explain why each function in Part 1 is an even function.

   b. Explain why the graph of any even function will have the same symmetry as the examples in Part 1.

4. Any function for which $f(-x) = -f(x)$ for all x is called an odd function.

   a. Explain why each function in Part 2 is an odd function.

   b. Explain why the graph of any odd function will have the same symmetry as the examples in Part 2.

A C E Homework starts on page 96.

5.2 Combining Profit Functions: Operating With Polynomials I

Amusement parks make money by charging for rides such as roller coasters, bumper cars, and water slides. They also make money from restaurants and stands that sell pretzels, ice cream, or lemonade. Profits of each type depend on the number of customers at the park.

Suppose that managers of the *Sahara Adventure Park* predict daily profit (in $100 units) as a function of the number of customers (in units of 100 customers) with two polynomial functions $R(n)$ and $F(n)$.

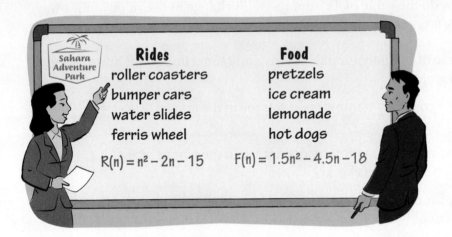

- What do the graphs of these functions look like?

- What do they tell about profit prospects for each part of the business?

- What single quadratic polynomial shows the total profit, $T(n)$, for the park on a day with n hundred customers?

- What single quadratic polynomial shows the difference in profit, $D(n)$, for the two sources of income on a day with n hundred customers?

Combining quadratic polynomials by addition and subtraction can provide information about profits at *Sahara Adventure Park*. Operations with those polynomials are similar to operations with multi-digit numbers.

Problem 5.2

A Explore the connection between polynomials and decimal numbers by answering the following questions.

1. Evaluate these expressions when $x = 10$.

   a. $5x$

   b. $3x^2$

   c. $4x^3$

   d. $7x^4$

   e. $6x^5$

   f. $6x^5 + 7x^4 + 4x^3 + 3x^2 + 5x + 8$

2. Write polynomial expressions for functions with these values.

   a. $p(10) = 2{,}357$

   b. $q(10) = 15{,}042$

   c. $r(10) = 754{,}302$

3. In part (2) you found $p(x)$ for which $p(10) = 2{,}357$ and $q(x)$ for which $q(10) = 15{,}042$.

   a. Write the rule for $r(x) = p(x) + q(x)$ as a single polynomial.

   b. Find the value of $r(10) = p(10) + q(10)$, using the expression in part (a).

4. How is adding decimal numbers like adding polynomials?

B Write each of these sums and differences of polynomials in standard polynomial form.

1. $(x^2 + 2x - 5) + (4x^2 - 7x + 12)$

2. $(x^2 + 2x - 5) - (4x^2 - 7x + 12)$

3. $(2x - 5) + (7x^2 + 3x + 4)$

4. $(2x - 5) - (7x^2 + 4)$

5. $(x^3 + 7x^2 + 3x + 4) + (-3x^4 - 7x^2 + 9)$

6. $(x^3 + 7x^2 + 3x + 4) - (-3x^4 - 7x^2 + 9)$

C What general strategy can be applied to find the sum or difference of two polynomials. How is that strategy justified?

continued on the next page >

Problem 5.2 *continued*

D Find the sum of the two quadratic profit functions $R(n)$ and $F(n)$ at *Sahara Adventure Park*. Use graphs and/or algebraic reasoning to answer these questions.

1. For what number of customers will the park have maximum total loss (i.e., minimum profit)? What is that loss?

2. According to the model, there is no maximum profit. Explain why this is true.

3. How many customers are needed for the park to break even ($0 profit)?

A C E Homework starts on page 96.

5.3 Product Time: Operating With Polynomials II

You can apply whole number arithmetic and properties of operations to develop an algorithm for polynomial multiplication.

Problem 5.3

A Calculate these number products. Be prepared to explain and justify the strategy you used in each case.

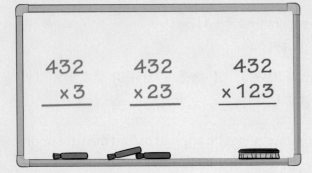

$$\begin{array}{r} 432 \\ \times\ 3 \\ \hline \end{array} \qquad \begin{array}{r} 432 \\ \times\ 23 \\ \hline \end{array} \qquad \begin{array}{r} 432 \\ \times\ 123 \\ \hline \end{array}$$

Problem 5.3

B **1.** Show why $(98)(70)$ is the same as $(100 - 2)(70)$.

2. Show why $(98)(73)$ is the same as $(100 - 2)(70 + 3)$.

C Write each of these products in simplest possible standard polynomial form. Be prepared to explain and justify the strategy you used in each case.

1. $(x^2 - 4)(7x)$

2. $(x^2 - 4)(7x + 3)$

3. $(2x - 5)(7x^2 + 3x + 4)$

4. $(x^3 + 6x^2 + 3x + 4)(7x^2)$

5. $(x^3 + 7x^2 + 3x + 4)(7x^2 + 9)$

6. $(x^2 + 3x + 4)(7x^2 + x - 2)$

D What general strategy can be applied to find the product of two polynomials? How is that strategy justified?

E The sum, difference, and product of any two integers is always another integer. Mathematicians say that the system of integers is closed under the operations of addition, subtraction, and multiplication. Is the same thing true of the system of polynomials? That is, will the sum, difference, or product of two polynomials always be another polynomial?

F **1.** Consider the case of $f(x) = (x^2 - 4)(x - 5)$, which has equivalent expression $f(x) = x^3 - 5x^2 - 4x + 20$. Which algebraic expression for the function makes it easier to predict these features of the graph?

    a. the y-intercept   **b.** the x-intercepts

2. **a.** Find the zeros of $f(x)$.   **b.** Sketch a rough graph of $f(x)$.

3. Consider the case of $g(x) = (x - 4)(x + 5)(x - 1)$, which has equivalent expression $g(x) = x^3 - 21x + 20$. Which algebraic expression for the function makes it easier to predict these features of the graph?

    a. the y-intercept   **b.** the x-intercepts

4. **a.** Find the zeros of $g(x)$.   **b.** Sketch a rough graph of $g(x)$.

A⟨**C**⟩**E** Homework starts on page 96.

5.4 The Factor Game Revisited

In Problem 1.1 of *Prime Time*, you played the *Factor Game* with small whole numbers. You have learned a lot of mathematics since this first Problem. Throughout *Connected Mathematics*, factoring with whole numbers and algebraic expressions has remained an important skill.

Playing the *Factor Game II* applies what you know about polynomial expressions. To play the game, you need a *Factor Game II* board and colored pens or markers.

Factor Game II

$x^3 + 5x^2 - 4x - 20$	$x - \sqrt{7}$	$x + 1$	$x^3 + 4x$	$x^3 + 3x - 10$
$4x^2 + 20x + 25$	$x + 2$	$x^4 - 16$	$x + 5$	$x^2 - 4$
$2x^2 + 9x + 10$	$x - 5$	$x - 2$	$x + \sqrt{7}$	$x - 2i$
$x^3 + 3x^2 + 3x + 1$	$2x + 5$	$x + 2i$	x	$x^2 - 10x + 25$
$x^4 - 14x^2 + 49$	$x^2 + 4$	$x^2 - 7$	$x^2 + 2x + 1$	$x^2 - 25$

Factor Game II

Rules

1. Player A chooses an expression on the game board and circles it.

2. Using the same color, Player A circles all the proper factors of Player A's expression.

3. Player B circles a new expression. Player B circles all of the factors that are not already circled.

4. The players take turns choosing expressions and circling factors.

5. If a player chooses an expression with no uncircled factors, that player loses their current turn and scores no points.

6. The game ends when there are no expressions left with uncircled factors.

7. Each player counts the number of expressions that he or she circled. The player with the greater total wins.

Problem **5.4**

Play the *Factor Game II* several times with a partner. Look for interesting patterns and strategies that might help you win. Make notes on your observations.

Ⓐ 1. Examine the *Factor Game II* board. For which polynomials are there no factors on the board? Explain how you know.

2. Which factor pairs are easy to recognize? Explain.

3. Are there factors on the board for which there is no product on the board?

4. For which polynomials is it most challenging to find factors? Explain.

Ⓑ Which polynomials are likely to have the most factors? Explain.

Ⓒ There are three cubic and two quartic polynomials on the board. What strategies did you use to decide on likely factors for these polynomials?

Ⓓ Is there a polynomial on the board that is *both* of the following?

• a factor of another polynomial on the board

• a product of two or more other polynomials on the board

Explain your reasoning.

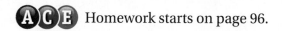 Homework starts on page 96.

Applications

For Exercises 1–5,

- Sketch a graph of the function for $-4 \le x \le 4$.
- Estimate coordinates of the local maximum or minimum point(s).
- Identify the intervals for x when the function values are increasing. Identify when the function is decreasing.
- Estimate coordinates for the x- and y-intercepts.

1. $f(x) = -0.1x^3 + 1$

2. $g(x) = 0.2x^4 - 10$

3. $h(x) = x^3 - x^2 - 2x$

4. $j(x) = -x^3 + x^2 + 2x + 5$

5. $k(x) = x^4 - 10x^2 + 9$

Write the sums and differences as equivalent standard polynomial expressions.

6. $(x^2 - x - 2) + (3x^2 + 5x + 10)$

7. $(3x^2 - 4x + 7) - (5x^2 - x)$

8. $(5x^3 + 3x^2 + 4x - 3) + (x^3 - 7x^2 - 4x + 1)$

9. $(x^3 - 7x^2 - 4x + 1) - (5x^3 + 3x^2 + 4x - 3)$

10. $(3x^3 + 5x^2 + 10) + (7x^4 + 5x^3 - 10x^2 + 4x)$

For Exercises 11–15 write the products as equivalent standard polynomial expressions.

11. $(3x + 4)(5x - 1)$

12. $(3x^2 + 5x + 10)(2x - 3)$

13. $(x^2 - x - 2)(3x^2 + 4x + 1)$

14. $(x^3 - 7x^2 - 4x + 1)(3x + 4)$

15. $(5x^3 + 3x^2 + 4x - 3)(x^2 + 7)$

Connections

16. If $c(x) = x^3$, find the values for $c^{-1}(x)$

   a. $c^{-1}(8)$ **b.** $c^{-1}(27)$

   c. $c^{-1}(-8)$ **d.** $c^{-1}(-64)$

17. If $q(x) = x^4$, find the values for $q^{-1}(x)$

   a. $q^{-1}(16)$ **b.** $q^{-1}(81)$

   c. $q^{-1}(1)$ **d.** $q^{-1}(-16)$

18. On a copy of the graph below, sketch graphs of these variations on the basic cubic function.

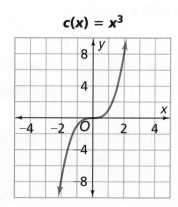

$c(x) = x^3$

   a. $f(x) = x^3 + 2$ **b.** $g(x) = (x - 2)^3$ **c.** $h(x) = 0.5x^3$

19. On a copy of the graph of $q(x) = x^4$ sketch graphs of these variations on the basic quartic function.

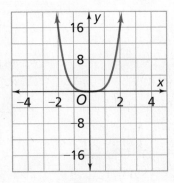

   a. $f(x) = x^4 - 5$

   b. $g(x) = (x + 1)^4$

   c. $h(x) = 0.2x^4$

20. In *Frogs, Fleas, and Painted Cubes*, you studied the number of colored faces on unit cubes that are assembled to make a larger cube with sides of length *n* whose 6 faces are then painted.

   a. Explain why the total number of unit cubes required to make such a larger cube with sides of length *n* must be n^3.

   b. Explain why the number of cubes with 3 painted faces is 8.

   c. Explain why the number of cubes with 2 painted faces is $12(n - 2)$.

   d. Explain why the number of cubes with only 1 painted face is $6(n - 2)^2$.

   e. Explain why the number of cubes with no painted faces is $(n - 2)^3$.

Extensions

21. Amami solved the quadratic equation $x^2 - 7x - 18 = 0$. His work is shown below.

$$x^2 - 7x - 18 = 0$$
$$(x + 2)(x - 9) = 0$$
$$x = -2 \text{ or } x = 9$$

    a. Why is the equation $x^2 - 7x - 18 = 0$ equivalent to $(x + 2)(x - 9) = 0$?

    b. How do you know that the equation $(x + 2)(x - 9) = 0$ has solutions -2 and 9?

    c. How can you check that $x = -2$ and $x = 9$ are solutions of $x^2 - 7x - 18 = 0$?

22. Larisa solved the equation $x^3 - 7x^2 - 18x = 0$. Her work is shown below.

$$x^3 - 7x^2 - 18x = 0$$
$$x(x^2 - 7x - 18) = 0$$
$$x = 0, \ x = -2 \text{ or } x = 9$$

    a. Why is the equation $x^3 - 7x^2 - 18x = 0$ equivalent to $x(x^2 - 7x - 18) = 0$?

    b. How do you know that the equation $x(x^2 - 7x - 18) = 0$ has solutions 0, -2, and 9?

    c. How can you check those solutions in the equation $x^3 - 7x^2 - 18x = 0$?

23. Use reasoning like that developed in Exercises 21 and 22 to solve these equations.

    a. $x^3 - 3x^2 + 2x = 0$

    b. $x^4 + 4x^3 + 3x^2 = 0$

    c. $x^3 - 9x = 0$

24. Write polynomial functions with these properties.

  a. $p(6) = 0$; $p(-1) = 0$; $p(0) = 0$

  b. $q(4) = 0$; $q(-3) = 0$; $q(7) = 0$

  c. $r(-3) = 0$; $r(-1) = 0$; $r(1) = 0$; $r(4) = 0$

  d. Anita, Cameron, and Ervin each drew a graph for part (c).

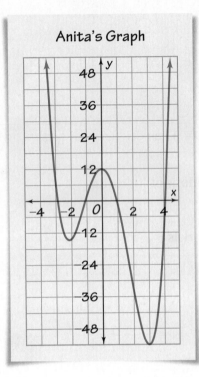

Anita's Graph

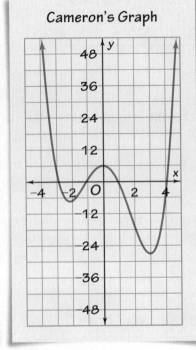

Cameron's Graph

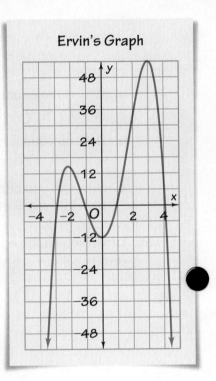

Ervin's Graph

How do you think Cameron's function rule is different from Anita's function rule? How do you think Ervin's function rule is different from Anita's function rule?

25. Use what you know about quadratic equations to solve polynomial equations of degree 4. In each case, apply the fact that $x^4 = (x^2)^2$.

  a. How do you know that the equation $x^4 - 16 = 0$ is equivalent to the equation $(x^2 + 4)(x^2 - 4) = 0$?

  b. How do you know that the only real number solutions of $(x^2 + 4)(x^2 - 4) = 0$ are 2 and -2? What complex number solutions are there for the equation?

  c. Solve $x^4 - 81 = 0$. Give both real and complex number solutions.

  d. How do you know that $x^4 - 5x^2 + 6 = 0$ is equivalent to $(x^2 - 3)(x^2 - 2) = 0$? What does that second equivalent equation tell you about the solutions to $x^4 - 5x^2 + 6 = 0$?

Mathematical Reflections 5

In this Investigation, you studied the properties of polynomial functions, expressions, and graphs. You developed strategies for adding, subtracting, and multiplying polynomial expressions. These questions will help you summarize what you have learned.

Think about your answers. Discuss your ideas with other students and your teacher. Then write a summary of your findings in your notebook.

1. **What** are polynomial expressions and functions?

2. **How** can one analyze the graph of a polynomial function $p(x)$ to discover

   a. solutions to the equations $p(x) = 0$?

   b. intervals on which values of the function are increasing or decreasing?

   c. points that show relative maximum or minimum values of the function?

3. **What** strategies give standard polynomial expressions for

   a. the sum or difference of two polynomials?

   b. the product of two polynomials?

Common Core Mathematical Practices

As you worked on the Problems in this Investigation, you used prior knowledge to make sense of them. You also applied Mathematical Practices to solve the Problems. Think back over your work, the ways you thought about the Problems, and how you used Mathematical Practices.

Elena described her thoughts in the following way:

We wanted to discover patterns in the graphs of degree 3 and 4 polynomials. It was helpful to have graphing software to test many examples.

We also wanted to develop algorithms for addition, subtraction, and multiplication of polynomials. It was important to recall connections to what we knew about decimal operations.

We also discovered that we could apply general properties of the number system to operations with polynomials.

....

Common Core Standards for Mathematical Practice
MP5 Use appropriate tools strategically.

 • What other Mathematical Practices can you identify in Elena's reasoning?

• Describe a Mathematical Practice that you and your classmates used to solve a different Problem in this Investigation.

Looking Back

In this Unit, you extended your understanding and skill in work with mathematical functions, expressions, equations, and graphs. You learned new function concepts such as domain, range, and inverses. You learned how to use $f(x)$ notation for describing functions.

You also studied examples of step, piecewise, and polynomial functions. You discovered the special properties of arithmetic and geometric sequences.

You saw how information about quadratic functions can be revealed by transforming graphs and writing expressions in vertex form. You developed a formula for solving any quadratic equation. Finally, you used that formula as a starting point for development of the complex number system.

Use Your Understanding: The Functions Five Game

Now it is time to test your understanding of those new mathematical ideas and techniques. Challenge yourself or other students in your class to play the Functions Five Game.

You will use game cards like the ones shown below. The cards have mathematical properties that you will match to functions.

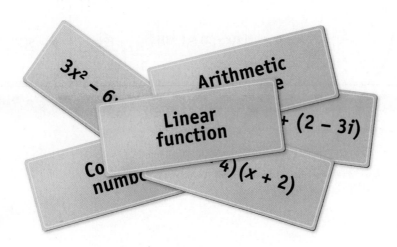

The Functions Five Game Board is shown below. You will match the properties on the cards to the functions in the cells. To make the property cards, write each of the properties listed on the facing page on a separate card. Then choose the game you want to play from the options described at the bottom of the facing page.

Game Board

$x^2 + 2bx + b^2$	$y = \sqrt[3]{x}$		$k(x) = \dfrac{3}{x}$	
$x = 1 \pm \sqrt{2}$	$f(n + 1) - f(n) = 3$	$5 - i$	$x^2 - 2x - 8$	
$j(x) = x^2 - 4x$	$(x - 1)^2 - 9$	$g(x) = -\frac{1}{3}y + \frac{2}{3}$		$x(x^2 - 1)$
$(3 + 2i) - (3i - 2)$		$v(x) = |x|$	$f(n + 1) \div f(n) = 3$	$y = -\frac{1}{3}x - \frac{2}{3}$
	$x \geq 0$	$x(x - 2) + (-8)$		$y = 5(3^{n-1})$

Properties

- Linear function
- Geometric sequence
- $g(x) = -(x + 2)^2 + 4$
- Degree 3 polynomial
- Inverse of $h(x) = -3x - 2$
- $(3 + 2i)(1 - i)$
- $(x - 4)(x + 2)$
- Arithmetic sequence
- Piecewise-defined function
- $3x^2 - 6x - 3 = 0$
- Perfect square trinomial
- $(x, y) \rightarrow (x - 2, y + 4)$
  for graph of $y = -x^2$
- Vertex form of a quadratic

- Complex number
- Step function
- Inverse of $y = x^3$
- $f(x) = (x - 2)^2 - 4$
- Quadratic function
- Domain of $r(x) = \sqrt{x}$
- $(3 + 2i) + (2 - 3i)$
- Inverse of $r(x) = \frac{3}{x}$
- Inverse variation function
- Formula for area of a square
- Exponential function
- $(x, y) \rightarrow (x + 2, y - 4)$
  for graph of $y = x^2$

Most cards can be matched with two or more cells on the game board. As a result, the Functions Five Game can be played in several different ways.

Rules

Option 1: Solitaire Study the game board and the set of game cards. Try to find a way to check off every cell on the board with the least number of cards.

Option 2: Five-by-Five Functions Each player or team picks a card and marks all of the cells on the game board that match the directions on the card. Then take turns. The winner is the player who has the most correct matches after each player has drawn five cards.

Option 3: Functions Five Follow the same directions as in Option 2. Play until one player or team has marked five cells in a row, column, or diagonal.

Option 4: Fickle Functions Follow the same directions as in Option 3. When a card is drawn, each player can only choose one corresponding cell on the game board that matches the directions on the card.

A **arithmetic sequence** A number sequence formed by adding a fixed number to each previous term to find the next term. The fixed number is called the common difference.

example 4, 7, 10, 13, . . .

progresión aritmética Una secuencia de números que se forma al sumar un número fijo a cada término anterior para hallar el siguiente término. El número fijo se conoce como diferencia común.

ejemplo 4, 7, 10, 13, . . .

C **compare** Academic Vocabulary
To tell or show how two things are alike or different.

related terms *analyze, relate*

sample Compare the graph of $f(x) = x^2$ with the graph of $g(x) = -(x - 2)^2 - 1$.

comparar Vocabulario académico
Decir o mostrar en qué se parecen y en qué se diferencian dos cosas.

términos relacionados *analizar, relacionar*

ejemplo Compara la gráfica de $f(x) = x^2$ con la gráfica de $g(x) = -(x - 2)^2 - 1$.

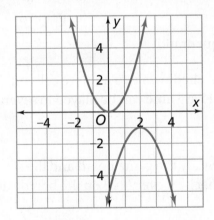

The graph of $g(x) = -(x - 2)^2 - 1$ has the same shape as $f(x) = x^2$. The graph of $g(x)$ is a vertical flip of the graph of $f(x) = x^2$, translated 2 units right and 1 unit down.

La gráfica de $g(x) = -(x - 2)^2 - 1$ tiene la misma forma que $f(x) = x^2$. La gráfica de $g(x)$ es una inversión vertical de la gráfica de $f(x) = x^2$, trasladada 2 unidades a la derecha y 1 unidad hacia abajo.

completing the square The process of writing any given quadratic expression in equivalent form $a(x - b)^2 + c$. Completing the square turns every quadratic equation into the form $(x - p)^2 = q$.

completar un cuadrado El proceso de escribir cualquier expresión cuadrática dada en la forma equivalente $a(x - b)^2 + c$. Cuando se completa un cuadrado, cualquier ecuación cuadrática a la forma $(x - p)^2 = q$.

complex conjugates Number pairs in the form $a + bi$ and $a - bi$ are complex conjugates.

conjugados complejos Los pares de números de la forma $a + bi$ y $a - bi$ son conjugados complejos.

complex numbers The set of numbers that can be written in the form $a + bi$ where a and b are real numbers and i is the number whose square is -1. 7, $6 + i$, and $-2i$ are examples of complex numbers.

números complejos El conjunto de números que se puede escribir en la forma $a + bi$, donde a y b son números reales e i es el número cuyo cuadrado es -1. 7, $6 + i$, y $-2i$ son ejemplos de numeros complejos.

D **degree of a polynomial** The highest power of the variable in monomial terms of the expression.

grado de un polinomio El grado más alto de la variable en términos monomios de la expresión.

describe Academic Vocabulary
To explain or tell in detail. A written description can contain facts and other information needed to communicate your answer. A diagram or a graph may also be included.

describir Vocabulario académico
Explicar o decir con detalle. Una descripción escrita puede contener datos y otro tipo de información necesaria para comunicar tu respuesta. También puede incluir un diagrama o una gráfica.

related terms *express, explain*

términos relacionados *expresar, explicar*

sample Describe how to calculate the nth term in the following sequence: $19, 11, 3, -5, -13, -21, \ldots$

ejemplo Describe cómo calcular el *enésimo* término en la siguiente progresión: $19, 11, 3, -5, -13, -21, \ldots$

The sequence $19, 11, 3, -5, -13, -21, \ldots$ is an arithmetic sequence with *common difference* -8. Using the formula $a_n = a_1 + (n - 1)d$, we can substitute 19 for a_1 and -8 for d. We now have $A_n = 19 + (n - 1)(-8)$, or more simply, $A_n = -8n + 27$, which finds the nth term.

La progresión $19, 11, 3, -5, -13, -21, \ldots$ es una progresión aritmética con la *diferencia común* -8. Usando la fórmula $a_n = a_1 + (n - 1)d$, podemos sustituir 19 por a_1 y -8 por d. Ahora tenemos $A_n = 19 + (n - 1)(-8)$, o de manera más simple, $A_n = -8n + 27$, que halla el *enésimo* término.

domain (of a relation or a function)
The set of possible values for the input or independent variable.

dominio (de una relación o una función)
El conjunto de valores posibles para la entrada o la variable independiente.

E **explain** Academic Vocabulary
To give facts and details that make an idea easier to understand. Explaining can involve a written summary supported by a diagram, chart, table, or a combination of these.

related terms *describe, show, justify*

sample Using the diagram below, explain why the expressions $x^2 + 4x + 3$ and $(x + 2)^2 - 1$ are equivalent.

explicar Vocabulario académico Dar datos y detalles que hacen que una idea sea más fácil de comprender. Explicar puede implicar un resumen escrito apoyado por un diagrama, una gráfica, una tabla o una combinación de estos.

términos relacionados *describir, mostrar, justificar*

ejemplo Usando el diagrama de abajo, explica por qué las expresiones $x^2 + 4x + 3$ y $(x + 2)^2 - 1$ son equivalentes.

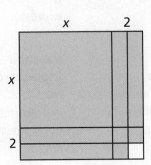

The diagram models $(x + 2)^2$ with a unit square missing from the right hand corner. The tiles in the diagram can be rearranged so that the length is $x + 3$ and the width is $x + 1$, which gives the area of $x^2 + 4x + 3$. Since the areas are equal, the expressions are also equivalent.

El diagrama representa $(x + 2)^2$ con una unidad cuadrada que falta en la esquina derecha. Los azulejos del diagrama se pueden volver a ordenar de manera que la longitud sea $x + 3$ y el ancho sea $x + 1$, que da el área de $x^2 + 4x + 3$. Dado que las áreas son iguales, las expresiones también son equivalentes.

F **function** A relationship between two variables in which the value of one variable depends on the value of the other variable.

función Una relación entre dos variables en la que el valor de una variable depende del valor de la otra.

function notation An expression in the form $f(x)$ that represents the value of the dependent variable when the independent variable is x. The notation is read 'f of x'.

notación de una función Una expresión en la forma $f(x)$ que representa el valor de la variable dependiente cuando la variable independiente es x. La notación se lee como "f de x".

function rule An equation that describes a function.

regla de la función Una ecuación que describe una función.

G **geometric sequence** A number sequence in which each term is multiplied by the same factor to find the next term.

example $9, 3, 1, \frac{1}{3}, \ldots$

progresión geométrica Una secuencia numérica en la que cada término se multiplica por el mismo factor para hallar el siguiente término.

ejemplo $9, 3, 1, \frac{1}{3}, \ldots$

I **imaginary number** Any number of the form bi, where b is a real number, and $b \neq 0$.

número imaginario Cualquier número de la forma bi, donde b es un número real y $b \neq 0$.

imaginary unit The complex number i whose square is -1.

unidad imaginaria El número complejo i cuyo cuadrado es -1.

inverse function If a function $f(x)$ pairs each input value a with a unique output value b, then the inverse of $f(x)$ is the function that pairs each b with a. The inverse of $f(x)$ is written as $f^{-1}(x)$.

If $f(x) = 3x + 2$, then $f^{-1}(x) = \frac{x - 2}{3}$ because, for example, $f(4) = 14$ and $f^{-1}(14) = 4$, and so on.

función inversa Si una función $f(x)$ empareja cada valor de entrada a con un valor de salida único b, entonces el inverso de $f(x)$ es la función que empareja cada b con a. El inverso de $f(x)$ se escribe como $f^{-1}(x)$.

Si $f(x) = 3x + 2$, entonces $f^{-1}(x) = \frac{x - 2}{3}$ porque, por ejemplo, $f(4) = 14$ y $f^{-1}(14) = 4$ y así sucesivamente.

L **local maximum** The value $f(k)$ of a function $f(x)$ that is greater than all other values of that function in some neighborhood of $x = k$. Local maximum points are represented by hilltops on graphs of $f(x)$. In the graph shown below, $(-1, 32)$ is a local maximum.

máximo local El valor $f(k)$ de una función $f(x)$ que es mayor que todos los demás valores de esa función en la vecindad de $x = k$. Los puntos máximos locales están representados por colinas en las gráficas de $f(x)$. En la gráfica que se muestra a continuación, $(-1, 32)$ es un máximo local.

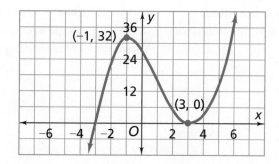

local minimum The value $f(x)$ of a function $f(x)$ that is less than all other values of that function in some neighborhood of $x = k$. Local minimum points are represented by valley bottoms on graphs of $f(x)$. In the graph shown above, $(3, 0)$ is a local minimum.

mínimo local El valor $f(x)$ de una función $f(x)$ que es menor que todos los demás valores de esa función en la vecindad de $x = k$. Los puntos mínimos locales están representados por fondos de valles en las gráficas de $f(x)$. En la gráfica que se muestra más arriba, $(3, 0)$ es un mínimo local.

P **piecewise-defined function** A function that has different rules for different parts of its domain.

función de fragmentos Una función que tiene reglas diferentes para diferentes partes de su dominio.

polynomial An algebraic expression in the form $a_n x^n + a_{n-1} x^{n-1} + \ldots + a_1 x^1 + a_0$, where n is a whole number and the coefficients a_n, a_{n-1}, a_1, and a_0 are numbers.

example $2x^2$, $3x + 7$, 28, and $-7x^3 - 2x^2 + 9$ are all polynomials.

polinomio Una expresión algebraica en la forma $a_n x^n + a_{n-1} x^{n-1} + \ldots + a_1 x^1 + a_0$, donde n es un número entero y los coeficientes a_n, a_{n-1}, a_1, y a_0 son números.

ejemplo $2x^2$, $3x + 7$, 28, y $-7x^3 - 2x^2 + 9$ son todos polinomios.

polynomial function A function with a rule represented in the form $f(x) = a_n x^n + a_{n-1} x^{n-1} + \ldots + a_1 x^1 + a_0$.

example $f(x) = x^3 + x^2 - 6x + 2$

función polinomial Una función con una regla representada en la forma $f(x) = a_n x^n + a_{n-1} x^{n-1} + \ldots + a_1 x^1 + a_0$.

ejemplo $f(x) = x^3 + x^2 - 6x + 2$

Q **Quadratic Formula** If $ax^2 + bx + c = 0$ and $a \neq 0$, then $x = \frac{-b}{2a} \pm \frac{\sqrt{b^2 - 4ac}}{2a}$.

fórmula cuadrática Si $ax^2 + bx + c = 0$ y $a \neq 0$, entonces $x = \frac{-b}{2a} \pm \frac{\sqrt{b^2 - 4ac}}{2a}$.

$$2x^2 + 10x + 12 = 0$$
$$x = \frac{-b}{2a} \pm \frac{\sqrt{b^2 - 4ac}}{2a}$$
$$x = \frac{-10}{2(2)} \pm \frac{\sqrt{10^2 - 4(2)(12)}}{2(2)}$$
$$x = \frac{-10}{4} \pm \frac{\sqrt{4}}{4}$$
$$x = \frac{-10}{4} + \frac{2}{4} \text{ or } x = \frac{-10}{4} - \frac{2}{4}$$
$$x = -2 \text{ or } -3$$

R **range (of a relation or a function)** The set of possible values for the output or dependent variable.

rango (de una relacion o funcion) El conjunto de los valores posibles para la salida o la variable dependiente.

represent Academic Vocabulary
To stand for or take the place of something else. Symbols, equations, charts, and tables are often used to represent particular situations.

related terms *symbolize, stand for*

sample Represent the table of values below as a graph and a function rule.

x	−3	−2	−1	0	1	2	3	4
y	6	1	−2	−3	−2	1	6	13

representar Vocabulario académico
Significar o tomar el lugar de algo más. Los símbolos, las ecuaciones, las gráficas y las tablas a menudo se usan para representar situaciones particulares.

términos relacionados *simbolizar, significar*

ejemplo Representa la siguiente tabla de valores como una gráfica y como una regla de la función.

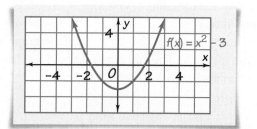

$f(x) = x^2 - 3$

S   **sequence** An ordered list of numbers that often forms a pattern.

progresión Lista ordenada de números que muchas veces forma un patron.

---

solving quadratic equations The process of finding the values of the variable that make the quadratic equation true. Methods for solving quadratic equations include factoring, completing the square, using the Quadratic Formula, and graphing.

resolver ecuaciones cuadráticas
El proceso de encontrar los valores de la variable que hacen que la ecuación cuadrática sea verdadera. Los métodos para resolver las ecuaciones cuadráticas incluyen descomponer en factores, completar un cuadrado, usar la fórmula cuadrática y hacer gráficas.

---

step function A function that pairs every number in an interval with a single value. The graph of a step function can look like the steps of a staircase.

función escalón Una función que empareja cada número de un intervalo con un solo valor. La gráfica de una función escalón se puede parecer a los peldaños de una escalera.

V vertex form The vertex form of a quadratic function is $f(x) = a(x - p)^2 + q$, where $a \neq 0$ and (p, q) is the coordinate of the vertex of the function.

example $f(x) = (x + 1)^2 - 2$
The vertex is $(-1, -2)$.

forma vértice La forma vértice de una función cuadrática es $f(x) = a(x - p)^2 + q$, donde $a \neq 0$ y (p, q) es la coordenada del vértice de la función.

ejemplo $f(x) = (x + 1)^2 - 2$
El vértice es $(-1, -2)$.

Z zeros of a function The values of x for which $f(x)$ is equal to 0. For example, the zeros of the function $f(x) = x^2 - 9$ are -3 and 3 because $f(-3) = 0$ and $f(3) = 0$. The zeros of a function are the x-intercepts of the graph of the function. The graph of $f(x) = x^2 - 9$ has x-intercepts at $(-3, 0)$ and $(3, 0)$.

ceros de una función Los valores de x para los que $f(x)$ es igual a 0. Por ejemplo, los ceros de la función $f(x) = x^2 - 9$ son -3 y 3 porque $f(-3) = 0$ y $f(3) = 0$. Los ceros de una función son los interceptos en x de la gráfica de una función. La gráfica de $f(x) = x^2 - 9$ tiene interceptos en x en $(-3, 0)$ y $(3, 0)$.

Index

Index

Acknowledgments

Cover Design

Three Communication Design, Chicago

Photographs

Photo locators denoted as follows: Top (T), Center (C), Bottom (B), Left (L), Right (R), Background (Bkgd)

003 iStockphoto/Thinkstock; **042** Christian Delbert/Shutterstock.